WILLIAMS-SONOMA

Christmas
ENTERTAINING

RECIPES AND TEXT

Georgeanne Brennan

GENERAL EDITOR

Chuck Williams

PHOTOGRAPHY

Quentin Bacon

FOOD STYLING

George Dolese

STYLING

Sara Slavin

*f*P
FREE PRESS

NEW YORK · LONDON · TORONTO · SYDNEY

CONTENTS

A REASON TO CELEBRATE

Christmas is a time of merriment and good cheer—a time when family and friends traditionally come together to celebrate. This book is designed to help you make the most of this festive season by encouraging you to invite people into your home to share a holiday cocktail or a simple meal.

For many of us, the idea of Christmas entertaining is a joyous one. But others find the prospect of hosting a party, whether an elaborate dinner or a simple breakfast, too stressful and time-consuming even to consider. After all, the party must be planned, the invitations sent, the decorations and menu decided, the house cleaned, the food prepared, the table set, and, of course, the guests greeted by a relaxed host. It is a tall order, but as you will discover in the pages that follow, it doesn't need to be a difficult one. Indeed, such celebrations can be enjoyable and worth the effort when you see the pleasure it brings your guests.

By careful planning, you can minimize stress and create a memorable occasion that centers on sharing the holiday spirit with friends, rather than struggling to be the consummate host. The more your entertaining reflects who you are, the more successful your entertaining will be and the more you will enjoy both the planning and the party.

This book offers tips for making your Christmastime entertaining enjoyable from beginning to end. You will find inspiration for six different celebrations, including menus, holiday beverages, and decorating ideas to help infuse your home and your table with a festive spirit. You can mix and match elements of these celebrations and add your own ideas as well, remembering that the best part of any Christmas gathering is spending time with family and friends.

PLANNING FOR CHRISTMAS

Your Christmas get-together will be rewarding if it is equally enjoyable for both you and your guests. To help you achieve that goal, here is a step-by-step guide to holiday entertaining to keep you organized and having fun from start to finish.

Reasons to Celebrate

The Christmas season offers countless opportunities for celebrating, from a casual breakfast to a formal Christmas dinner to a lively cocktail party. The first step is to decide what type of holiday celebration you would like to host.

Choosing a Style

Next, determine the overall style of your gathering. This involves deciding on whether you envision a casual or formal affair, the timing of the party, the menu and how it will be served, and details like decorations, lighting, and seating.

Begin by deciding who will be on the guest list. Once you know how many people you are inviting, you can fix the time of the event and decide whether you want a cozy or a free-flowing ambience. These choices will help you settle on the style of serving and a color palette that will create the desired mood. Also consider the weather. In a warm climate, you might want to serve Christmas drinks on the deck, followed by a buffet inside. In a cold climate, you may opt for cocktails near the fireplace and a formal supper in the dining room. In every case, you will want to fill the house with seasonal decorations such as candles, ornaments, and fragrant greenery.

Casual entertaining is about being comfortable and relaxed while enjoying simply prepared food, typically served on a buffet or family style at the table. It's an ideal setting when children are included because they have freedom to come and go, while adults can enjoy themselves at a more leisurely pace. For even greater flexibility, you can set up a separate seating area for the children, outfitting it with whimsical decorations and clever gifts. For a touch of elegant informality, serve passed appetizers and drinks before you sit down at the table.

Formal entertaining often signifies a memorable event and is particularly well suited for holiday dinners. A formal table is generally refined and elegant, with the menu served in several courses that are usually plated in the kitchen or at a sideboard. Fine linens and your best china dress the table, which also tends to include a carefully arranged seasonal centerpiece. A seating plan is usually used. Remember, though, formality does not mean stiffness, and elegance does not mean stuffiness. Even the most formal setting should be comfortable and welcoming for your guests.

HOSTING A HOLIDAY COOKIE EXCHANGE

Gather friends to share their best baking secrets and stockpile holiday cookies.

- Three weeks before the party, draw up the guest list, send invitations, and decide on the menu. Ask guests to bring one dozen cookies for each person invited, a tray for displaying their cookies, containers for carrying cookies home, and copies of their recipe.

- One week before the party, find out what cookies guests are bringing to prevent any duplicates.

- Two days before the party, bake your cookies and shop for your menu.

- On the day of the party, decorate a table with Christmas greenery and ornaments and prepare your menu. As guests arrive, ask them to display their cookies on the table, and then serve your menu.

- During the party, exchange recipes and help guests pack up their cookies to take home.

Planning a Christmas Menu

Part of the fun and success of Christmas entertaining is careful menu planning. Here is where you can be at your most creative, pulling together ideas about the kind of meal and dining experience you want your guests to have with the space and time you have available. The type of party you are hosting sets the tone for the food. And although holidays often call for traditional recipes, there are lots of ways to infuse your menu planning with new ideas.

Be realistic. For starters, consider the size of your guest list—Christmas celebrations often include extended family and out-of-town visitors—and how much time and space you have. These three factors will guide your menu planning and style of service for the celebration.

Decide on a theme. Christmas is rich in food traditions from many cultures, giving you a wealth of choices. You might focus on your own regional or ancestral heritage or on that of a special guest or of a country that interests you, or you can celebrate with a mix of traditions.

Think seasonally. Visit a local farmers' market for a close-up look at the variety of seasonal fruits, vegetables, and specialty products, including wreaths, cut flowers, and potted plants.

Ask for help. If your Christmas calendar is busy and you're pressed for time, don't hesitate to ask for help with the cooking or decorating from one or more of your guests. This only adds to the holiday spirit and will relieve some of the pressure of preparing everything on your own.

Choosing Beverages

Christmas is an ideal time to serve a festive beverage, such as a citrus cocktail or hot mulled wine, with the appetizers, followed by wine with the meal. Include a few festive nonalcoholic offerings, such as sparkling cider or a cranberry spritzer. When calculating wine, plan for one bottle for every two or three drinkers. Choose easy-to-prepare beverages, chill bottles and glasses, and have garnishes ready before the party.

Serving Styles

With your guest list set and your menu chosen, you can now pick a service style to match. No matter which one you choose, welcome your guests with drinks and appetizers to launch the celebration.

Buffet service works well for large or small gatherings and is ideal for more casual events like an open house. The food is presented in bowls and on platters, usually on a sideboard or table, and guests serve themselves. Chafing dishes, warming trays, and the like can be used to keep hot foods at the correct temperature. All you have to do is replenish platters and bowls as needed. If space allows, set up a separate self-service drinks area and dessert station.

Family-style service is ideal for less formal Christmas meals and smaller groups, where platters and bowls can be comfortably passed at the table. Choose serving ware that is small enough to be handled easily, and consider having duplicate platters at each end of the table to shorten distances. Wine and water can be placed directly on the table and passed as well.

HOLIDAY-PLANNING CHECKLIST

Planning ahead will help you stay organized and relaxed during the holidays.

- Decide on the type of get-together
- Determine the number of guests
- Set a time and a location in your house
- Send out invitations (one month prior)
- Choose an entertaining style
- Plan a doable menu that fits the style
- Pick a color palette
- Select your decorations
- Shop for nonperishable items well ahead of the date
- Decorate your space and set the table at least one day in advance

Restaurant-style service, in which the food is individually plated in the kitchen, or served by the host at the table and then passed to the guests, is formal and stylish but can require more last-minute work than other service styles. It is a good option for intimate Christmas dinners and works well when the menu features several courses. Water and wine can be placed on the table or on a sideboard.

Cocktail parties are a fun way to welcome a large group into your home and can be particularly festive during the holidays. They traditionally start in the early evening and last a few hours. The food is generally passed on trays, with bowls of nuts, olives, or other snacks set on a coffee table or on small tables around the room for easy access. For a particularly large party, you might want to set up a drink station with a server to make cocktails and keep beverages flowing smoothly. Even with a tended drink station, consider setting aside a different area where guests can serve themselves wine, beer, and sparkling water.

Setting the Holiday Scene

The mood of the party and the expectations of the guests are set by subtle but important elements like seating arrangements, lighting, decorations, and other special touches. For inspiration, look through the six celebrations described in this book, each of which sets a distinctive scene.

Seating. Christmas celebrations are usually a time when people who don't have the opportunity to see one another often are able to get together. In order to encourage conversation, arrange intimate seating areas where guests can sit and chat, either before dinner or during a cocktail party. At the table, mix and match chairs to accommodate your group—even a bench or the piano stool can be pressed into service. If you are making a seating plan, position your more gregarious guests next to those who are quieter to balance the conversation, and outfit each place setting with a place card. If any guests have special needs, make sure you have planned sufficiently in advance how to accommodate them gracefully.

Lighting. Use floor lamps, table lamps, and mass groupings of candles to create soft, flattering pools of light. Dim or turn off overhead lights. For nighttime celebrations, a strand of small Christmas lights strung along a banister or the edge of a fireplace mantel creates a holiday sparkle and adds to the festive spirit. When setting the table with candles, use tall tapers, votives or shorter pillars, or a mixture.

Centerpieces. The Christmas centerpiece is an opportunity to show off the season's regalia, from holiday ornaments and colorful fruits to boughs of greenery and pine cones. It can be as simple as a white platter laden with holiday greens and berries, with silver ornaments and tiny gold paper–wrapped gifts tucked in among the greens, or a red-berry wreath set on a platter with the center filled with ivory candles of different sizes. A centerpiece can also incorporate meaningful items, such as native plants, Christmas heirlooms, or family memorabilia. In every case, make sure your centerpiece is low enough and positioned so guests can see over it with ease.

Special touches. Christmas celebrations offer the perfect opportunity to add extra flourishes. These can be small decorative details, such as a miniature bouquet of holiday greens and berries tied to the back of each chair, or a take-home seasonal offering, such as a bottle of wine or a tin of cookies. When children are present, consider putting a small gift at each place setting or making a special holiday beverage—perhaps cranberry juice mixed with sparkling water—just for them.

Staying Organized

Behind every successful party is a well-organized host who has drawn up a number of lists according to category, checked off items as they were completed, and carefully planned ahead so that little is left to chance. To ensure a smooth celebration, start your planning earlier than you think necessary.

Making lists. Make a separate list for each of your Christmas gatherings, and divide each list into three additional lists: food and drinks, decorations, and a timeline. On the first list, write down the ingredients you need to purchase for the recipes you are making. For special items, such as a prime rib or wines and spirits, include notes on where you will buy them and if they must be ordered in advance. On the decorations list, include such items as wreaths, place cards, and candles. Finally, make a detailed timeline for each meal, working backward from the moment of serving to the initial days of preparation. Use the work plans that accompany each celebration in this book to help you put together your timeline.

Planning ahead. Check all of your linens, glassware, tableware, flatware, serving dishes, and kitchen equipment well in advance of the party date to make sure you have everything you need. Write down anything you lack, and plan to buy, borrow, or rent it. If you will be serving your meal buffet style, arrange empty platters and bowls on the table to be certain everything fits. Stock up on colorful Christmas napkins for snacks and appetizers—you almost always need more than you think—and any new holiday decorations you have decided to acquire.

CHRISTMAS GIFTS FROM THE KITCHEN

While cookies and candies are always welcome at Christmastime, here are some additional ideas for gifts from the kitchen:

- Pack mixed dried herbs, such as rosemary and lavender, in a colorful drawstring bag with an identifying tag and a recipe for using them.

- Make infused oils or vinegars, put them in pretty bottles, affix labels, and wrap with tissue paper and a ribbon.

- Prepare a special jam, such as quince or blackberry. Attach a tag with serving suggestions, tied with a ribbon that complements the jam color.

- Create a boxed sampler of several miniature loaf cakes that reflect the season, such as cranberry, persimmon, orange, walnut, and dried apricot. Line the box with colorful tissue paper.

Wine and Holiday Entertaining

Matching a single wine with the multitude of flavors that make up a holiday feast can be challenging. A good solution is to offer both a white and a red, so guests can enjoy either or both. If you are unsure about selecting wines, bring your menu to a trusted wine merchant or a wine-savvy friend for advice.

When pairing wine with a holiday cheese selection, aim for three or four varieties of cheese, such as a fresh goat's milk cheese, a blue cheese, a Brie, and an aged sheep's milk cheese. These flavors will marry nicely with Pinot Noir, Cabernet Sauvignon, Chardonnay, and Sauvigon Blanc.

Ideally, each place setting includes a different glass for each wine you will be serving. A tulip-shaped white-wine glass and a larger, similarly shaped red-wine glass are most versatile. If limited to a single type of glass, a large white-wine glass is the most versatile choice. Stemless wineglasses add a festive touch. For sparkling wines, use tall flutes, which enhance effervescence.

Once guests are seated, fill glasses one-third full. Serve sparkling wines well chilled (42°–45°F/6°–7°C) as an aperitif, with the first course, or throughout the meal. Chill whites to 45°–50°F (7°–10°C), and serve reds and dessert wines at cool room temperature.

A Holiday to Remember

Paying special attention to details like colorful decorations, lighting, and small gifts for guests to take home will send your friends and family out the door brimming with happy Christmas memories, while choosing the menu and the service style in advance and with care will help to ensure your meal perfectly suits the occasion. Such planning is the key to success. The six holiday parties that follow, each accompanied by seasonal menus, planning tips, and easy-to-follow decoration and style ideas, are your stepping-stones to memorable Christmas entertaining for years to come.

MATCHING HOLIDAY FOOD AND WINE

HOLIDAY FOOD	WINE MATCH
Appetizers and savory snacks	Sparkling wines *Champagne, Prosecco, California sparkling wine*
Turkey	Crisp whites or spicy, medium-bodied reds *Chardonnay, Sauvignon Blanc, Zinfandel, Syrah, Pinot Noir*
Ham or other smoked meats	Fruity, medium-bodied white or red wines *Riesling, Gewürztraminer, Pinot Gris, Pinot Noir*
Roasted red meats like prime rib	Full-bodied reds *Cabernet Sauvignon*
Rich foods such as creamed soups	Full-bodied white or red wines *Chardonnay, Merlot, Cabernet Sauvignon, Zinfandel, Syrah*
Acidic foods such as salads	High-acid white or red wines *Sauvignon Blanc, Zinfandel, Chianti*
Desserts	Sweet white or red wines that taste as sweet as the dish *Sauternes, Vin Santo, Muscat*
Double- or triple-crème cheeses	Sweet or fruity white or red wines *Sauternes, young Pinot Noir, tawny Port*
Blue-veined cheeses	Sweet white or red wines *Oloroso sherry, Sauternes, Port*

FIRESIDE COCKTAIL PARTY

A low table placed in front of a blazing fire and set with glass vases of flowers and citrus, colorful napkins, and a selection of hors d'oeuvres provides a focal point for a cozy Christmas cocktail party. By serving the finger food in courses, beginning with a series of bite-sized appetizers and followed by heartier fare and then dessert, guests will enjoy the sense of a complete meal without the formality.

Little is needed for decoration beyond the glow of the fire. Consider setting out a bowl filled with fresh fruits, their leaves still attached, and slipping small gift boxes, each wrapped in colorful paper, under the Christmas tree.

MENU

Iced Vin de Citron

Lemon Vodka Martinis

— • —

*Brioche Rounds with Crème Fraîche
and Golden Caviar*

Golden Beets with Smoked Trout and Dill

Skewers of Scallop Ceviche

Pecorino Gougères with Prosciutto

*Roasted Lamb Chops with
Rosemary and Sea Salt*

— • —

Chocolate Frangelico Truffles

Candied Grapefruit Peel

TIPS FOR A FESTIVE COCKTAIL PARTY

- Keep overhead lights low and string small holiday lights along the fireplace.

- Use glass vases and bowls to catch and reflect the fire and lights.

- Garnish serving plates and tables with seasonal citrus, olives, pine, and cedar.

- Tuck wrapped gifts beneath the tree.

- Use bright-colored cocktail napkins.

WORK PLAN

AT LEAST ONE DAY IN ADVANCE

Make the *gougères* and prepare their filling

Cook and slice the beets

Candy the grapefruit peel

Make the truffles

THE DAY OF THE PARTY

Make the vin de citron

Make the brioche rounds

Marinate the scallops

Assemble the beet and trout appetizers

Assemble the *gougères*

JUST BEFORE SERVING

Chill the cocktail glasses

Finish the skewers

Cook the lamb chops

Assemble crème fraîche and
caviar appetizers

use a bar-style lemon stripper to remove a strip of peel about 4 inches (10 cm) long from a lemon. Repeat until there is no more peel on the lemon, then repeat with 6 or 7 more lemons until you have 24 strips.

tie each strip of peel in a loose, single knot, to create 24 knots.

place a knot in each compartment of two 12-well ice-cube trays, fill with water, and freeze until solid.

ICED VIN DE CITRON

In this refreshing nonalcoholic cocktail, lemon cuts the sweetness of grape juice, and mint provides a touch of color and a hint of flavor. The recipe can be doubled and made ahead in a pitcher, and then poured over ice to serve.

4 cups (32 fl oz/1 l) white grape juice, chilled

3/4 cup (6 fl oz/180 ml) fresh lemon juice

Lemon zest ice cubes (optional, recipe at left)

8 fresh mint sprigs for garnish

Chill 8 glasses in the freezer for 15 minutes.

Pour 1/2 cup (4 fl oz/125 ml) grape juice into each chilled glass, add 1 1/2 tablespoons lemon juice, and 3 ice cubes. Garnish each glass with a mint sprig.

Serves 8

LEMON VODKA MARTINIS

The use of lemon vodka makes it a snap to prepare this cocktail, but unflavored vodka could be used instead—simply rub the glass with a lemon wedge before adding the liquor. Caper berries make an interesting and flavorful garnish.

Ice cubes

2 cups (16 fl oz/500 ml) lemon vodka, chilled

8 teaspoons dry vermouth, or to taste

8 caper berries, with stems intact, for garnish

Chill 8 martini glasses in the freezer for 15 minutes.

For each serving, put several ice cubes in a cocktail shaker and add 1/4 cup (2 fl oz/60 ml) of the vodka and 1 teaspoon or less of the vermouth. Shake vigorously and strain into a chilled martini glass. Garnish with a caper berry.

Serves 8

BRIOCHE ROUNDS WITH CRÈME FRAÎCHE AND GOLDEN CAVIAR

Brioche bread is very tender and light and makes perfect toasts for delicate toppings. If you cannot find brioche, thin-sliced sandwich bread is a good alternative. Use fancifully shaped cookie cutters if desired.

Preheat the oven to 400°F (200°C). Have ready an ungreased large baking sheet.

Using a $1^1/_2$-inch (4-cm) round or shaped biscuit cutter, cut 4 rounds from each bread slice. Arrange the rounds on the baking sheet. Bake until lightly golden, about 12 minutes. Turn the toasts over and bake until the second side is golden, about 10 minutes longer. Set aside.

When ready to serve, spread each toast with about $1/_2$ teaspoon of the crème fraîche, top with a little caviar, and garnish with a light sprinkle of chives.

Serves 14–16

15 thin slices brioche or white sandwich bread

$3/_4$ cup (6 oz/185 g) crème fraîche

$1^1/_2$ oz (45 g) golden caviar or salmon roe

$1/_4$ cup ($1/_3$ oz/10 g) cut-up fresh chives (1-inch/2.5-cm lengths)

GOLDEN BEETS WITH SMOKED TROUT AND DILL

The beets can be cooked and sliced the day before—then all that is required the day of the party is quick assembly. Red beets can be used as well, but they will tint the edges of the cream cheese pink.

Preheat the oven to 350°F (180°C).

Put the beets in a shallow baking dish, drizzle with the olive oil, and sprinkle with the salt. Turn to coat well. Roast until the beets are easily pierced with the tines of a fork, about 80 minutes. Let cool.

Slip off the skins and slice the beets into rounds $1/_4$ inch (6 mm) thick. Top each slice with about $1/_2$ teaspoon cream cheese, a piece of trout, and a sprinkle of dill. If desired, put each assembled round atop a cracker. Arrange on a platter and serve.

Serves 14–16

12 small golden beets, each $1^1/_2$–2 inches (4–5 cm) in diameter

2 tablespoons extra-virgin olive oil

1 teaspoon sea salt

4 oz (125 g) cream cheese, at room temperature, or crème fraîche

1 smoked trout fillet, about 5 oz (155 g), broken into bite-sized pieces

$1/_4$ cup ($1/_3$ oz/10 g) minced fresh dill

2 packages water crackers for serving (optional)

Skewers of Scallop Ceviche

1 1/4 lb (625 g) sea scallops, thawed if frozen

1/4 cup (1/3 oz/10 g) minced fresh cilantro (fresh coriander), plus 1 bunch for garnish

1 jalapeño chile, seeded and minced (about 2 tablespoons)

1/2 teaspoon salt

2 teaspoons peeled and grated fresh ginger

Grated zest of 1 lime

1/2 cup (4 fl oz/125 ml) fresh lime juice

1 1/2 tablespoons minced red onion

1 small tomato, peeled, seeded, and minced

1 lime, sliced, for garnish

Sea scallops, which are bigger than the bay variety, are ideal for this dish. Look for skewers made of interesting materials in kitchen-supply stores; in this case, bamboo with a decorative knot at the end. Serving the skewers on a bed of cilantro creates a festive presentation.

Rinse and dry the scallops and cut horizontally into slices 1/4 inch (6 mm) thick. Thread the scallop pieces onto wooden skewers, using 5 scallop slices per skewer. Arrange the skewers in a single layer in a shallow nonreactive dish and sprinkle with the minced cilantro, 1 tablespoon of the minced chile, the salt, ginger, and lime zest. Carefully pour the lime juice over the scallops and turn the skewers several times. The scallops should be covered by the juice. Cover with plastic wrap and refrigerate for at least 3 hours and up to 12 hours before serving, turning occasionally.

About 30 minutes before serving, sprinkle the scallops with the remaining chile, the onion, and the tomato. Turn the skewers several times.

To serve, using the bunch of cilantro, make a bed on a platter and arrange the scallop skewers on top. Garnish with the lime slices and serve.

Serves 14–16

Pecorino Gougères with Prosciutto

These savory puffs are made with pâte à choux, *or puff paste, and then sliced open and filled with delicate shavings of cheese and prosciutto.*

Preheat the oven to 425°F (220°C). Line 2 baking sheets with parchment (baking) paper and set aside.

In a saucepan over medium-high heat, combine 1 cup (8 fl oz/250 ml) water, the butter, salt, white pepper, and cayenne. Bring to a boil, stirring, and continue to cook until the butter is melted, 2–3 minutes. Add the flour and mix vigorously with a wooden spoon until a thick paste forms and pulls away from the side of the pan, about 3 minutes. Remove from the heat and make a well in the center. Crack 1 egg into the well and beat it into the hot mixture, using the wooden spoon or an electric handheld mixer. Repeat with 3 more eggs, beating them in one at a time, and adding the 2 tablespoons of finely grated cheese along with the fourth egg.

Fit a pastry bag with a $^1/_2$-inch (12-mm) round tip and spoon about half of the egg mixture into it. Pipe the mixture onto the prepared baking sheets into rounds 1–1$^1/_2$ inches (2.5–4 cm) in diameter and about $^1/_2$ inch (12 mm) high, spacing them 2 inches (5 cm) apart. Repeat with the remaining half of the mixture. You should have 30 rounds in all. (Alternatively, use a teaspoon to shape the *gougères*. Dip the spoon into a glass of cold water, then scoop up a generous teaspoon of the mixture and push it onto the baking sheet with your fingertips. Repeat, dipping the spoon in the water each time to prevent sticking.) In a small bowl, lightly beat the remaining egg. Brush the top of each *gougère* with a little of the beaten egg.

Bake for 10 minutes, then reduce the oven temperature to 350°F (180°C) and bake until the *gougères* are golden brown and crunchy, about 15 minutes longer. Do not underbake, or they will be mushy. When done, pierce each *gougère* with a wooden skewer, turn off the oven, and leave them in the oven for 10 minutes. Remove from the oven and let cool for at least 30 minutes on the baking sheets before filling.

Cut the prosciutto slices into 30 pieces. Using a vegetable peeler, shave the cheese into thin pieces. Cut each *gougère* in half and tuck in a folded piece of prosciutto and some shavings of cheese. They should look plump and generously filled.

Serves 14–16

6 tablespoons (3 oz/90 g) unsalted butter

1 teaspoon salt

$^1/_2$ teaspoon freshly ground white pepper

Pinch of cayenne pepper

1 cup (5 oz/155 g) all-purpose (plain) flour

5 large eggs

2 tablespoons finely grated *pecorino romano* cheese, plus 4-oz (125-g) block for shaving

3 oz (90 g) very thinly sliced prosciutto

ROASTED LAMB CHOPS WITH ROSEMARY AND SEA SALT

Racks of lamb are roasted and then cut into individual chops. You can serve the bite-sized chops as a casual finger food or offer small plates, knives, and forks. For an elegant presentation, ask your butcher to french the ribs—trim off the fat between each chop to expose the tips of the bones.

4 racks of lamb, each 1¹/₂–1³/₄ lb (750–875 g) with 7 or 8 ribs, frenched (see note)

4 cloves garlic, bruised

2 tablespoons coarse sea salt

4 teaspoons freshly ground pepper

4 tablespoons (2 fl oz/60 ml) olive oil

2 tablespoons finely chopped fresh rosemary, plus several sprigs for garnish

Preheat the oven to 475°F (245°C). Place 2 roasting pans, each large enough to hold 2 racks of lamb, in the oven. (Alternatively, use 4 baking dishes each large enough to hold a single rack of lamb.)

Rub the lamb and bones with the garlic cloves. Rub all over with the salt and pepper.

In each of 2 large, nonstick frying pans over medium heat, warm 2 tablespoons of the olive oil. When the oil is hot, add 2 of the lamb racks, fat side down, to each pan and sear for 1–2 minutes. Using tongs to turn and hold the lamb, sear both ends, about 1 minute on each end. Finally, sear the bone side for 1–2 minutes.

Transfer the lamb to a platter or cutting board and sprinkle all over with the chopped rosemary. Cover the exposed bones with aluminum foil to keep them from charring. Place the racks, bone side down, in the warmed roasting pans. Roast until an instant-read thermometer inserted into the thickest part of the meat (but not touching bone) registers 130°–140°F (54°–60°C) for medium-rare, 13–15 minutes; or 140°–150°F (60°–65°C) for medium, 15–20 minutes.

Transfer the lamb to a cutting board and tent loosely with aluminum foil. Let rest for 7–10 minutes.

To serve, cut the racks into chops and arrange the chops on a warmed platter. Garnish with the rosemary sprigs.

Serves 14–16

CHOCOLATE FRANGELICO TRUFFLES

Homemade truffles are easy to make and can be prepared up to two weeks in advance. In this recipe, they receive a double dose of hazelnut flavoring, in the liqueur and in the nut coating. Keep the truffles in the freezer until just before serving. For a fuller, dark chocolate taste, use bittersweet chocolate in place of the semisweet.

8 oz (250 g) semisweet (plain) chocolate

1/2 cup (4 fl oz/125 ml) heavy (double) cream

2–3 teaspoons Frangelico liqueur

1/2 cup (1 1/2 oz/45 g) unsweetened cocoa powder

1/2 cup (2 oz/60 g) finely ground hazelnuts (filberts)

Cut the chocolate into 1-inch (2.5-cm) pieces. Place in the top pan of a double boiler set over (but not touching) gently simmering water. Stir as the chocolate melts. When it is melted, stir in the cream, mixing well.

Remove the top pan from the heat and let the chocolate cool until nearly firm, 2–3 hours. Stir the Frangelico into the cooled chocolate.

Line a tray or baking sheet with parchment (baking) paper or aluminum foil. Using a melon baller, scoop out rounds of chocolate, arranging them on the tray. When all the chocolate has been used, cover the chocolate balls with aluminum foil and place the tray in the freezer for at least 30 minutes or for up to 2 weeks.

A day or so before serving, remove the truffles from the freezer. Place the cocoa powder in a small shallow bowl and the ground nuts in a second bowl. Roll the frozen balls first in the cocoa and then in the hazelnuts, coating them evenly each time and handling them as little as possible. As each ball is coated, return it to the tray. Then return the tray to the freezer.

About 15 minutes before serving, remove the tray from the freezer and arrange the truffles on a serving platter or tray.

Makes about 40 truffles; serves 14–16

CANDIED GRAPEFRUIT PEEL

Grapefruit peel becomes mild when cooked in several changes of water, and then absorbs a sugar syrup in a final cooking before being rolled in sugar. These candied peels can be made several days ahead and stored in an airtight container.

Using a sharp knife, cut a thin slice from the top and the bottom of each grapefruit. From the top to the bottom, score through the outer peel and thick white pith to the flesh inside, spacing the cuts about 1 inch (2.5 cm) apart. Peel the grapefruits. Cut each peel section lengthwise into long strips $1/4$ inch (6 mm) wide. (Reserve the flesh for another use.)

Put the peels in a large saucepan and add water to cover by 2 inches (5 cm). Bring to a boil over medium-high heat and cook for 10 minutes. Drain off the cooking water and repeat 2 more times, using fresh water each time. The peel will begin to soften and become translucent.

2 grapefruits, ruby or other variety

$2^1/2$ cups ($1^1/4$ lb/625 g) sugar

In another saucepan, combine $1^1/2$ cups (12 fl oz/375 ml) water with $1^1/2$ cups (12 oz/375 g) of the sugar. Bring to a boil over high heat and stir to dissolve the sugar, 3–4 minutes. Add the peels, reduce the heat to low, and simmer, uncovered, until the peels are translucent and much of the syrup has been absorbed, about 10 minutes.

Using a slotted spoon, transfer the peels to a sheet of aluminum foil, arranging them in a single layer. Let dry for 3–4 hours. Sprinkle the remaining 1 cup (8 oz/250 g) sugar on another sheet of foil and roll the peels in the sugar to coat well. Set aside and let dry for a few hours longer. The peels should be supple but not limp.

Arrange the peels in layers in an airtight container, separating each layer with a piece of waxed paper. Store in a cool, dry place until serving.

Makes about 3 dozen pieces; serves 14–16

ITALIAN CHRISTMAS EVE

Christmas Eve dinner in Italian households is noted for its bountiful array of fresh seafood, its selection of good wines, and the celebratory spirit of the guests. Even if you're not Italian, you can create the joyful mood of this family party with large platters and bowls, subtle hints of red and green in the decorations, and an Italian-inspired cocktail. Provide your guests with oversized napkins, and

use colorful, painted pottery for tableware. Incorporate branches of olives or fresh herbs into your centerpiece and fill the air with Christmas carols sung in Italian, or arias from such favorite works as Rigoletto *and* Così fan tutte.

TIPS FOR AN ITALIAN HOLIDAY DINNER

- Incorporate a few pieces of Italian Deruta ware, known for its vibrant colors and designs, into your table setting for an authentic touch.

- Serve the dinner family style in the spirit of the typical Italian family table.

- Choose serving dishes that are ample enough to hold a half-dozen servings.

- Finish the meal with foil-wrapped chocolates imported from Italy, served with espresso.

MENU

Campari and Soda

Antipasto Platter

*Mâche with Walnut Oil and
Balsamic Vinaigrette*

Stuffed Cherry Peppers

— • —

Lemon Risotto

Shrimp, Scallops, and Stuffed Squid

Arugula, Radicchio, and Escarole Salad

— • —

*Ricotta Cheesecake with
Blood Orange Marmalade Glaze*

WORK PLAN

AT LEAST ONE DAY IN ADVANCE

Stuff the peppers

Make the shallot and tomato sauce
and the stuffing for the squid

Make the cheesecake

THE DAY OF THE PARTY

Marinate the shrimp

Make the dressings for the salads

Arrange the antipasto platter

Stuff the squid

JUST BEFORE SERVING

Chill the aperitif glasses

Make the risotto

Finish the seafood dish

Toss the salads

place 2 or 3 ice cubes in each glass, pour the Campari over them, and add the soda.

stir the Campari and soda together with a spoon or swizzle stick until well mixed.

garnish each glass with a strip of orange or lemon peel, and arrange the glasses on a tray or platter.

CAMPARI AND SODA

Campari is a popular aperitif created in the 1860s by Gaspare Campari, a bartender in Milan. Aficionados favor the bright red drink for its complex taste reminiscent of bitter oranges, one of its components. It is typically served with soda.

12–18 ice cubes

1¹/₂ cups (12 fl oz/375 ml) Campari

1 bottle (16 fl oz/500 ml) soda water, or as needed, chilled

Thin slices of orange or lemon peel for garnish

Chill 6 glasses in the freezer for 15 minutes.

In each glass, place 2 or 3 ice cubes and pour in ¹/₄ cup (2 fl oz/60 ml) of the Campari. Add ¹/₃ cup (3 fl oz/80 ml) of the soda water, or more to taste, stir, and garnish with a citrus peel.

Serves 6

ANTIPASTO CENTERPIECE

An inviting platter of antipasti begins an Italian holiday meal and sets the tone for the courses that follow. Beautifully arranged and bountiful, it is easy to assemble and sure to be a crowd pleaser.

select a tray or platter large enough to hold the bowls and small dishes of the individual items, and then plan your arrangement.

fill each of the serving vessels with a different antipasto item, with an eye toward keeping the mix of colors balanced.

garnish the filled platter with olive sprigs or other greenery, such as fir or cedar.

place the antipasto platter in the center of the table so that guests can admire it before sitting down to the meal.

ANTIPASTO PLATTER

A large platter of antipasti opens the meal with an abundance of flavors, colors, and textures, including a salad and pickled cherry peppers, allowing guests to compose their own first course. Any Italian cured meats can be substituted for the soppressata *and* coppa.

$1/2$ lb (250 g) *coppa* dry salami, thinly sliced and skin removed

$1/2$ lb (250 g) *soppressata* salami, thinly sliced and skin removed

1 cup (4 oz/125 g) walnut halves

2 cups (10 oz/315 g) mixed olives such as picholine, Kalamata, Niçoise, and oil cured, in any combination

Stuffed Cherry Peppers (page 45)

Mâche with Walnut Oil and Balsamic Vinaigrette (page 45)

Arrange the cured meats, walnuts, olives, stuffed cherry peppers, and salad in various bowls and plates and place on a large platter or tray. Alternatively, serve the meats and walnuts on one platter, pair the olives and stuffed peppers on a second platter, and offer the salad on a third platter or in a bowl.

Serves 6

MÂCHE WITH WALNUT OIL AND BALSAMIC VINAIGRETTE

Mâche is a delicate salad green favored throughout Europe, including Italy. It has a slightly nutty flavor that is complemented by walnut oil. Look for a first-pressed walnut oil; after it is opened, store it in the refrigerator and use within six months.

Leave the small florets of mâche intact and separate the larger ones.

In the bottom of a salad bowl, using a fork, gently mix together the walnut oil, vinegar, salt, and white pepper. Add the mâche but do not toss. Just before serving, gently turn to coat the mâche. Serve at once as part of the antipasto platter.

Serves 6

4–5 cups (4–5 oz/125–155 g) mâche

3 tablespoons walnut oil

2 teaspoons balsamic vinegar

$1/2$ teaspoon fine sea salt

$1/4$ teaspoon freshly ground white pepper

STUFFED CHERRY PEPPERS

Red and green pickled cherry peppers are often part of an antipasto platter, but here they are stuffed with a savory filling of provolone, prosciutto, and capers. These can be entirely prepared in advance. If you can't find cherry peppers, peperoncini *also work well.*

Cut off the top from each pepper about a third of the way down. Reserve the tops. With a small spoon, scoop out and discard the seeds from the center of each pepper. Set the peppers aside.

In a bowl, mix together the bread crumbs, cheese, prosciutto, pine nuts, and capers. Add 3 tablespoons of the olive oil and mix. Continue to add olive oil until the mixture just holds together. Season to taste with salt and pepper.

Fill each pepper with some of the stuffing mixture, mounding it on the top. Top each stuffed pepper with a reserved top. Serve as part of the antipasto platter.

Serves 6

$1^1/2$ jars (each 1 lb/500 g) pickled sweet cherry peppers, drained

$1^1/2$ cups (3 oz/90 g) fresh bread crumbs

$1/4$ lb (125 g) provolone cheese, minced

2 oz (60 g) prosciutto, minced

$1/4$ cup ($1^1/2$ oz/45 g) pine nuts, chopped

3 tablespoons capers, rinsed, drained, and chopped

4–5 tablespoons (2–$2^1/2$ fl oz/60–75 ml) extra-virgin olive oil

Salt and freshly ground pepper

LEMON RISOTTO

This creamy risotto is especially good served with fish. Be sure to add the lemon zest at the end, so its flavor will be fresh and bright; its volatile oils will quickly dissipate if warmed too long.

3 cups (24 fl oz/750 ml) chicken stock or reduced-sodium chicken broth

5 tablespoons (2$^1/_2$ oz/75 g) unsalted butter

3 tablespoons extra-virgin olive oil

3 tablespoons minced shallots

2$^1/_4$ cups (1 lb/500 g) Arborio rice

$^1/_2$ cup (4 fl oz/125 ml) fresh lemon juice

$^1/_4$ cup ($^1/_3$ oz/10 g) coarsely grated lemon zest

$^3/_4$ cup (3 oz/90 g) freshly grated Parmesan cheese, plus shaved cheese for garnish

Salt

$^1/_4$ cup ($^1/_3$ oz/10 g) minced fresh chervil (optional)

In a saucepan over high heat, combine the chicken stock and 3$^1/_2$ cups (28 fl oz/875 ml) water and bring to a boil. Reduce the heat to low and maintain a simmer.

In another saucepan over medium heat, melt 2 tablespoons of the butter with the olive oil. Add the shallots and sauté until translucent, 2–3 minutes. Add the rice and stir until it is opaque, about 3 minutes. Add about $^3/_4$ cup (6 fl oz/180 ml) of the simmering stock, adjust the heat to maintain a simmer, and cook, stirring, until most of the stock is absorbed, about 3 minutes. Continue adding the stock, about $^3/_4$ cup at a time and stirring constantly, until all but about $^1/_2$ cup (4 fl oz/125 ml) of the stock has been used, the rice is nearly tender and still slightly firm in the center, and the mixture is creamy, 20–25 minutes.

Add the lemon juice to the remaining $^1/_2$ cup stock and add the mixture, little by little, to the rice along with the remaining 3 tablespoons butter, the lemon zest, and the grated Parmesan, always stirring constantly. Taste for salt and add as needed.

If desired, stir in the chervil. Transfer to a serving bowl, garnish with shavings of Parmesan, and serve at once.

Serves 6

Shrimp, Scallops, and Stuffed Squid

The squid can be stuffed and refrigerated several hours before cooking, and the sauce can be made the morning of the dinner.

To make the shrimp, in a bowl, combine the shrimp, olive oil, lemon juice, garlic, salt, ground pepper, and red pepper flakes. Cover and refrigerate for 1 hour.

Preheat the broiler (grill). Remove the shrimp from the marinade, reserving the marinade, and lay them on a broiler pan. Broil (grill) 4–5 inches (10–13 cm) from the heat source, brushing twice with the marinade, until opaque throughout, 5–7 minutes. Transfer to a warmed platter and sprinkle with the parsley.

To make the scallops, dry well and season with the salt and pepper. In a large frying pan over medium-high heat, melt the butter with the olive oil. When hot, add the scallops and sear, turning once, until golden, about 30 seconds on each side. Pour in the wine and scrape up any browned bits. Add the vinegar and turn the scallops once more to cook through, about 1 minute total. Transfer to a warmed platter.

To make the squid, pat the whole bodies dry and mince the tentacles; set aside. In a large saucepan over medium heat, warm 2 tablespoons of the olive oil. Add the shallots and sauté until translucent, about 4 minutes. Add half of the basil and the tomatoes and their juice and cook, stirring occasionally, until thick, about 20 minutes. Season with salt and pepper and stir in the remaining basil. Set aside.

In a frying pan over medium-high heat, heat 2 tablespoons of the olive oil. Add the onion and sauté until nearly translucent, about 2 minutes. Add the spinach and stir until wilted, about 2 minutes. Add the tentacles and bread crumbs and stir until the tentacles are opaque and the crumbs are lightly golden, about 4 minutes longer. Stir in the prosciutto, season with salt and pepper, and let cool. Pack 2–3 teaspoons into each squid body and close with a toothpick.

In a large frying pan over medium heat, warm the remaining 2 tablespoons olive oil. When hot, add the stuffed squid in a single layer and sauté, turning as needed, just until opaque, 4–5 minutes. Transfer to a warmed platter. Reheat the sauce and pour over the squid, serving the extra alongside. Serve all the seafood at once either on a single, large platter or on separate platters.

Serves 6

SHRIMP

36 large shrimp (prawns), peeled and deveined

1/4 cup (2 fl oz/60 ml) extra-virgin olive oil

3 tablespoons fresh lemon juice

2 cloves garlic, minced

1 teaspoon salt

1/2 teaspoon freshly ground pepper

1/4 teaspoon red pepper flakes

2 teaspoons chopped fresh flat-leaf (Italian) parsley

SCALLOPS

18 sea scallops

1 teaspoon fine sea salt

1/2 teaspoon freshly ground pepper

1 teaspoon unsalted butter

2 1/2 teaspoons extra-virgin olive oil

1/3 cup (3 fl oz/80 ml) dry white wine

1 teaspoon balsamic vinegar

SQUID

18 small squid, each 3–4 inches (7.5–10 cm) long, cleaned

6 tablespoons (3 fl oz/90 ml) extra-virgin olive oil

2 large shallots, minced

1/4 cup (1/3 oz/10 g) minced fresh basil

1 can (28 oz/875 g) plum (Roma) tomatoes, coarsely chopped, with juice

Salt and freshly ground pepper

1 yellow onion, minced

4 cups (8 oz/250 g) chopped spinach

1/4 cup (1/2 oz/15 g) fresh bread crumbs

1/4 cup (2 oz/60 g) minced prosciutto

Arugula, Radicchio, and Escarole Salad

Radicchio and escarole are both members of the chicory family and mildly bitter. Arugula is slightly peppery and combines well with these two distinctive components to make a classic Italian salad.

In the bottom of a salad bowl, using a fork, gently mix together the olive oil, red wine vinegar, and balsamic vinegar. Mix in the sea salt.

Add the arugula, radicchio, escarole, and parsley leaves but do not toss. Just before serving, toss to coat the greens with the vinaigrette. Serve at once.

Serves 6

1/4 cup (2 fl oz/60 ml) extra-virgin olive oil

1 tablespoon red wine vinegar

2 teaspoons balsamic vinegar

1/2 teaspoon sea salt

1 cup (1 oz/30 g) baby arugula (rocket) leaves

1/2 head radicchio, torn into bite-sized pieces

1 head escarole, pale yellow inner leaves only, torn into bite-sized pieces

1/2 cup (1/2 oz/15 g) fresh flat-leaf (Italian) parsley leaves

RICOTTA CHEESECAKE WITH BLOOD ORANGE MARMALADE GLAZE

Ricotta gives this cake an added creaminess, and garnet-hued blood orange marmalade makes a flavorful topping.

Preheat the oven to 325°F (165°C).

To make the crust, in a food processor, finely chop the cookies and transfer to a bowl. Finely grind the walnuts with the sugar and add to the ground cookies. Add the melted butter and mix well until the dry ingredients are evenly moistened. Transfer the crumb mixture to a 9-inch (23-cm) springform pan and, using your fingers, cover the bottom and about 1¹/₂ inches (4 cm) up the sides of the pan. Bake until lightly browned, about 15 minutes. Let cool on a wire rack for 10 minutes, then place in the freezer. Reduce the oven temperature to 300°F (150°C).

To make the filling, in a blender or food processor, combine the cream cheese, ricotta, orange zest, sugar, vanilla, egg yolks, cream, and salt. Process until smooth, 1–2 minutes. Pour into a large bowl. In another bowl, using an electric mixer on high speed, beat the egg whites until stiff peaks form. Using a spatula, fold about ¹/₃ of the egg whites into the cheese mixture and stir to incorporate. Then, gently fold in the remaining egg whites just until incorporated.

Remove the crust from the freezer and pour the cheese mixture into it, smoothing the top. Bake for 30 minutes. Raise the oven temperature to 325°F (165°C) and continue to bake until the surface is golden and the edges are firm but the center still jiggles, 30–35 minutes longer. Turn off the oven, open the oven door, and let the cheesecake cool in the oven for about 3 hours. The center will fall slightly. Cover tightly with plastic wrap, being careful not to let the wrap touch the surface. Refrigerate for at least 12 hours or up to overnight.

To make the orange topping, in a small saucepan over low heat, combine the marmalade and 2–3 tablespoons of water and heat to melt the marmalade. Set aside until cool, then spread on top of the cheesecake, creating an even layer of glaze. Garnish with the orange zest. Release and remove the pan sides and place the cheesecake on a serving plate. To serve, cut into wedges with a sharp knife, dipping it into water and wiping it dry after each cut.

Serves 6–8, with leftovers

CRUST

6 oz (185 g) gingersnap cookies

1¹/₄ cups (5 oz/155 g) walnuts

¹/₄ cup (2 oz/60 g) sugar

5 tablespoons (2¹/₂ oz/75 g) unsalted butter, melted

FILLING

8 oz (250 g) cream cheese, at room temperature, cut into 4 pieces

7 oz (220 g) whole-milk ricotta, drained well

Grated zest of 1 orange

1 cup (8 oz/250 g) sugar

1 teaspoon vanilla extract (essence)

4 large eggs, separated

²/₃ cup (5 fl oz/160 ml) heavy (double) cream

¹/₈ teaspoon salt

BLOOD ORANGE MARMALADE TOPPING

¹/₂ cup (5 oz/155 g) blood orange or regular orange marmalade

Shredded zest of 1 orange

CHRISTMAS EVE
IN THE CITY

A candlelit Christmas Eve captures the sparkle of bustling city life with a festive sit-down dinner featuring a lavish multicourse menu. Putting the dining table alongside a large window incorporates the lights of the cityscape into your holiday decorations and gives your guests a dazzling view while they sip aperitifs.

Use the unexpected and understated palette of ice blue, silver, and white to enhance the cool elegance of this cosmopolitan menu and set the tone for the evening. In the rest of the room, keep the decorations restrained so as not to draw attention away from the beauty of the table.

MENU

Champagne Cocktails

Belgian Endive Tipped with
Crème Fraîche, Capers, and Ahi Tuna

— • —

Shrimp Bisque

— • —

Crab Salad with Green Apples
and Grapefruit Coulis

— • —

Beef Tenderloin with Shallot and
Syrah Reduction

Twice-Cooked Potatoes

— • —

Almond and Apple Tart

TIPS FOR AN ELEGANT
HOLIDAY DINNER

- Set the table and decorate the room with silver and crystal for a sparkling, twinkling ambience.

- Use groups of candles of different shapes and sizes on the table and throughout the space to create enough soft light to illuminate the room.

- Pass the appetizers on trays for a more formal, elegant presentation.

- Select music ahead of time and load the CD player, so you won't need to rise from dinner to make adjustments.

WORK PLAN

AT LEAST ONE DAY IN ADVANCE

Start the bisque

Cook the potatoes

Make the tart pastry

THE DAY OF THE PARTY

Prepare the Belgian endive appetizers

Finish the bisque

Assemble the crab salad and
grapefruit coulis

Finish the tart

JUST BEFORE SERVING

Chill the Champagne glasses

Cook the tenderloin and make the sauce

Finish the potatoes

purchase a ready-made, shimmery table runner in a color that matches your party palette, or buy fabric and hem or tape to size.

intermingle crystal candleholders and votives along the runner. Add candles that match or complement the palette, and place silver stars near the light to provide glitter.

place floral arrangements down the center of the table; make them low so that guests can see one another across the table.

A SHIMMERY TABLE

A rich, layered table setting is created when an ice-blue shimmery runner is laid lengthwise down the center of the table, and then decorated with a collection of glittering silver stars or other ornaments. The sparkling effect is heightened further by the addition of flickering candlelight and intimate bouquets of winter-white flowers.

CHAMPAGNE COCKTAILS

For a truly festive beginning to the evening, offer Champagne cocktails with a variety of liqueurs. Chambord, which is raspberry, is popular in French restaurants, as is crème de cassis, or black currant, the basis of the Kir Royale. Crème d'amandes is more unusual, with a subtle almond flavor; amaretto could be used instead.

Chill 8 Champagne flutes in the freezer for 15 minutes.

Pour about 1 tablespoon liqueur into each glass. Fill with Champagne and serve.

Serves 8

1/2 cup (4 fl oz/125 ml) Chambord, crème de cassis, or crème d'amandes

2 bottles (24 fl oz/750 ml each) Champagne or sparkling wine

BELGIAN ENDIVE TIPPED WITH CRÈME FRAÎCHE, CAPERS, AND AHI TUNA

This elegant appetizer combines pure, simple flavors. When choosing heads of Belgian endive, look for those that are pale yellow on the tips; these are the freshest and mildest. For the tuna, select sashimi grade.

Cut 1/2 inch (12 mm) off the stem end of each head of Belgian endive. Separate the leaves. Choose 40 of the largest leaves (reserve the smaller ones for another use).

Put a dollop of crème fraîche at the base of each Belgian endive leaf to cover about a third of the leaf. Add a sprinkle of the diced tuna and a few capers, arranging them artfully over the crème fraîche. Cover and refrigerate until serving.

Serves 8

6 heads Belgian endive (chicory/witloof)

1 cup (8 oz/250 g) crème fraîche

1/2 lb (250 g) sashimi-grade ahi tuna, finely diced

5 tablespoons (2 1/2 oz/75 g) capers, rinsed, drained, and patted dry

SHRIMP BISQUE

5 fresh thyme sprigs

5 fresh flat-leaf (Italian) parsley sprigs

1 small yellow onion, quartered

1 small carrot, peeled and quartered

8 peppercorns

2 bay leaves

1¹/₂ lb (750 g) shrimp (prawns), preferably with heads intact

¹/₃ cup (3 fl oz/80 ml) extra-virgin olive oil

1 bottle (24 fl oz/750 ml) Sauvignon Blanc

1 teaspoon fine sea salt

4 cups (32 fl oz/1 l) heavy (double) cream

Freshly ground pepper

The secret to this soup is making a simple stock from the shrimp cooking water, and then reducing the stock with the sautéed shrimp shells to concentrate the rich flavors.

In a large, heavy-bottomed saucepan or Dutch oven, combine 6 cups (48 fl oz/1.5 l) water, the thyme, parsley, onion, carrot, peppercorns, and bay leaves. Bring to a boil over medium-high heat. Add the shrimp and cook just until they turn opaque, 1–2 minutes. Using a slotted spoon, transfer the shrimp to a colander and rinse them under cold running water. Reduce the heat to low so the stock simmers.

Cover and refrigerate 8 shrimp in the shell. Peel the remaining shrimp, reserving the heads and shells. Coarsely chop the shrimp, cover, and refrigerate.

In a frying pan over medium-high heat, warm the olive oil. When hot, add all the shrimp heads and shells and sauté for 5–8 minutes. Reduce the heat to medium and continue to sauté for 15 minutes. Add the contents of the pan to the simmering stock and cook until reduced to about 2 cups (16 fl oz/500 ml), about 45 minutes. Using the slotted spoon, remove the herbs, vegetables, and shells and heads and discard. Add the wine, raise the heat to high, and bring to a boil. Reduce the heat to low and simmer, uncovered, until reduced to about 3 cups (24 fl oz/750 ml), 30–40 minutes. Add the salt. (The soup can be made up to this point a day ahead, cooled, and refrigerated. Bring to a simmer over medium heat before continuing.)

Add the cream, raise the heat to medium-high, and heat, stirring, until small bubbles form along the edge of the pan. Reduce the heat to medium and simmer, stirring frequently, until the soup is reduced to about 4 cups (32 fl oz/1 l) and is thick and creamy, about 20 minutes. Taste and adjust the seasoning with salt. Strain the soup through a chinois, a fine-mesh sieve, or cheesecloth (muslin). Pour into a clean saucepan and heat over medium heat, stirring, until small bubbles form along the edge of the pan. Remove from the heat and cover.

In a saucepan over low heat, gently reheat the chopped and whole shrimp. To serve, divide the chopped shrimp equally among warmed soup bowls. Ladle ¹/₂ cup (4 fl oz/125 ml) of the soup into each bowl. Float a whole shrimp in the center of each bowl and sprinkle with freshly ground pepper. Serve at once.

Serves 8

CRAB SALAD WITH GREEN APPLES AND GRAPEFRUIT COULIS

Here, the apples are cut into matchsticks with a mandoline, but a sharp knife could be used as well. The syruplike grapefruit coulis, slightly sweetened, can be drizzled on top or in a border around the crab.

Using a sharp knife, cut a slice from the top and bottom of the grapefruit to reveal the flesh. Stand the grapefruit upright on a cutting board and thickly slice off the peel and white pith in strips, following the contour of the fruit. Holding the grapefruit in one hand, cut along either side of each segment to release it from the membrane, letting the segments drop into a bowl. Set 2 grapefruit segments aside. Coarsely chop the rest of the segments.

In a saucepan, combine the chopped grapefruit with $1/4$ cup (2 fl oz/60 ml) water. Bring to a boil over medium-high heat, reduce the heat to low, and simmer, stirring, until soft, about 5 minutes. Purée in the pan with an immersion blender or transfer the mixture to a stand blender to purée. Strain the purée through a fine-mesh sieve into a clean saucepan. Add the sugar and bring to a boil over medium-high heat, stirring. Continue to cook, stirring, until a syrup forms and the liquid is reduced by about half, 3–4 minutes. Remove from the heat and let cool.

Fill a bowl with water and add the lemon juice. Cut the apples into quarters lengthwise, and core the quarters. Place in the acidulated water to prevent discoloring. Using the julienne attachment on a mandoline, julienne the apples, and return them to the acidulated water. Alternatively, julienne with a knife.

In a bowl, combine the crabmeat, olive oil, vinegar, 2 tablespoons of the chives, the salt, black pepper, and cayenne. Pat dry half of the apples and add them to the bowl. Squeeze 2 teaspoons juice from the reserved grapefruit segments into the bowl. Turn gently to mix, being careful not to shred the crab.

To serve, divide the crab salad evenly among 8 salad plates, mounding it on each plate. Pat dry the remaining apples and divide them evenly among the salads, arranging them in a small stack on top. Spoon about 2 teaspoons of the grapefruit coulis in a thin line around the edge of each salad. To finish, sprinkle the remaining 1 tablespoon chives evenly over the salads.

Serves 8

1 grapefruit

2 teaspoons sugar

Juice of 1 lemon

2 Granny Smith apples

1 lb (500 g) fresh-cooked lump crabmeat, picked over for cartilage and shell fragments

3 tablespoons extra-virgin olive oil

$1^{1}/_{2}$ tablespoons white wine vinegar or Champagne vinegar

3 tablespoons minced fresh chives

$1/_2$ teaspoon fine sea salt

$1/_2$ teaspoon freshly ground black pepper

Pinch of cayenne pepper

1 beef tenderloin, 2¹/₂–3 lb
(1.25–1.5 kg)

2 tablespoons extra-virgin olive oil

2 teaspoons minced fresh thyme

1¹/₂ teaspoons fine sea salt

1 teaspoon freshly ground pepper

2 tablespoons minced shallots

1 cup (8 fl oz/250 ml) Syrah

2¹/₂ tablespoons unsalted butter

Beef Tenderloin with Shallot and Syrah Reduction

The tenderloin is the most tender cut of beef and is the source of the filet mignon. It needs only relatively brief cooking. The Syrah reduction, made from the flavorful pan juices, is quickly made while the roast rests.

Preheat the oven to 450°F (230°C).

Rub the beef all over with the olive oil, then rub on the thyme, salt, and pepper.

Place the roast on a rack in a shallow roasting pan just large enough to accommodate it. Roast until an instant-read thermometer inserted into the thickest part of the meat registers 115°–120°F (46°–49°C) for rare, about 20 minutes; 125°–130°F (52°–54°C) for medium-rare, about 25 minutes; or 130°–140°F (54°–60°C) for medium, about 30 minutes.

When the roast is the desired degree of doneness, transfer to a cutting board and tent loosely with aluminum foil. Let rest for about 15 minutes.

Meanwhile, remove the rack from the roasting pan and place the pan on the stove top over medium heat. Add the shallots and sauté, stirring them into the pan juices, until translucent, about 2 minutes. Add the wine a little at a time, stirring and scraping up any browned bits from the bottom of the pan. Continue to cook until the wine is reduced by nearly half. Stir in the butter. When the butter has melted, remove from the heat and cover to keep warm.

To serve, cut the beef into slices ¹/₂ inch (12 mm) thick. Arrange the slices on a warmed platter and drizzle with the sauce. Serve at once.

Serves 8

Twice-Cooked Potatoes

Here, the potatoes are first boiled and cooled, then they are sliced and sautéed in butter and olive oil, where they develop a golden crust. The first cooking can occur up to a day in advance, allowing you to prepare them ahead and finish right before serving.

Put the potatoes and 1 tablespoon of the salt in a large pot and add water to cover by 3 inches (7.5 cm). Bring to a boil over high heat, reduce the heat slightly, and cook until tender when pierced with the tines of a fork, 30–35 minutes. Do not overcook. Drain the potatoes and, when cool enough to handle, peel them. Let cool completely, and then cut into slices 1/2 inch (12 mm) thick. Cover and refrigerate until ready to do the second cooking.

In a large frying pan over medium-high heat, melt the butter with the olive oil. When hot, place the potato slices in the pan in a single layer, sprinkle them with half of the remaining salt, and cook until golden on the first side, 7–8 minutes. Turn the slices, sprinkle with the remaining salt, and cook until golden on the second side, about 5 minutes.

Using a slotted spatula, transfer to paper towels to drain briefly. Serve hot.

Serves 8

8–10 Yukon gold or white potatoes

2 tablespoons coarse sea salt

2 tablespoons unsalted butter

3 tablespoons extra-virgin olive oil

ALMOND AND APPLE TART

Tackle this tart in stages to serve at the end of an elegant holiday dinner. The pastry can be prepared up to one week ahead, and the almonds can be toasted and ground in a food processor up to four days in advance.

To make the pastry, in a food processor, combine the flour, sugar, and salt and pulse 4 times. Add the butter and pulse 10–12 times until the mixture is the size of small peas. Add the ice water and pulse again just until absorbed. Press a bit of the dough together. If it will not hold, add 1–2 teaspoons more ice water and pulse again. Press into a ball; it will be crumbly. Place between 2 sheets of plastic wrap and press down to make a disk about 1 inch (2.5 cm) thick. Refrigerate for 24 hours.

Preheat the oven to 400°F (200°C). Have ready a 9½-inch (24-cm) tart pan with a removable bottom. With the dough still between the sheets of plastic wrap, roll it out into a round 12–13 inches (30–33 cm) in diameter and ¼ inch (6 mm) thick. Return it to the refrigerator and chill for 10 minutes. Remove the plastic wrap and press the dough round into the tart pan. Trim off the overhang. Line the shell with aluminum foil and fill with pie weights. Bake until the edges are pale gold, about 15 minutes. Remove from the oven and remove the weights and foil. Prick the bottom with a fork, return to the oven, reduce the heat to 350°F (180°C), and bake until the bottom is pale gold, 5–10 minutes longer. Let cool on a wire rack.

To make the filling, in a saucepan, combine the apples, Calvados, ½ cup (4 oz/125 g) of the sugar, the salt, and water just to cover. Bring to a boil over medium-high heat and cook, stirring to dissolve the sugar, for 10 minutes. Remove from the heat and let the apples cool in the liquid for 30 minutes. In a bowl, stir together the almonds, the remaining ½ cup sugar, and the almond extract. In another bowl, using an electric mixer, beat together the butter and egg until fluffy. Gently mix in the cream and stir in the almond-sugar mixture.

Remove the apples from the poaching liquid, reserving the liquid, and slice ¼ inch (6 mm) thick. Pour the cream mixture into the tart shell. Top with the apple slices in concentric circles. Bake until a toothpick inserted into the center comes out clean, about 30 minutes. Let cool on a wire rack. Boil the poaching liquid over high heat until reduced to ¼ cup (2 fl oz/60 ml), and then brush over the tart. Let cool for at least 30 minutes, sprinkle with cinnamon, if using, and serve with ice cream.

Serves 8–10

TART PASTRY

1¼ cups (6½ oz/200 g) all-purpose (plain) flour

1 teaspoon sugar

½ teaspoon salt

½ cup (4 oz/125 g) chilled unsalted butter, cut into small pieces

2 tablespoons ice water, or as needed

FILLING

3 large Golden Delicious apples, peeled, halved, and cored

1 cup (8 fl oz/250 ml) Calvados

1 cup (8 oz/250 g) sugar

¼ teaspoon salt

1 cup (5½ oz/170 g) whole natural almonds, toasted and finely ground

⅛ teaspoon almond extract (essence)

5 tablespoons (2½ oz/75 g) unsalted butter, at room temperature

1 large egg

2 tablespoons heavy (double) cream

Coarsely ground cinnamon (optional)

Honey or vanilla ice cream for serving

NEW ENGLAND CHRISTMAS

This traditional Christmas dinner gives a nod to the old country with a gleaming, polished table pulled close to a roaring fire and a menu that includes favorites like eggnog, roast beef, and a steamed pudding—although local lobster and smoked salmon have their roles to play, too. Have friends help with the preparations by assigning a dish to each guest. The theme of simplicity and warmth

is carried out in the decorations, with a commanding centerpiece of candles and greenery arranged on a platter and napkins tied with glittering tree ornaments. Off-white candles, in candelabras and tucked between clusters of red berries and pine boughs, illuminate the sideboard and mantel and cast the room with a welcoming glow.

TIPS FOR A CLASSIC CHRISTMAS DINNER

• Incorporate branches of holly or berries into a centerpiece mixed with stocky candles in different heights.

• Display a bowl of presents wrapped in shiny foil, holiday baubles, or seasonal hard candies.

• Decorate the mantel and sideboard with greenery, berries, and tall candles.

• Choose recipes that don't require too much last-minute attention.

MENU

Eggnog with Nutmeg and Cinnamon

Smoked Salmon and
Watercress Cream on Toast Points

Roquefort and Walnut Puff Pastry Rolls

— • —

Lobster Salad with Tarragon and
Champagne Vinaigrette

— • —

Standing Rib Roast
with Garlic-Peppercorn Crust

Herbed Yorkshire Pudding

Braised Brussels Sprouts with Sage Butter

Creamy Gratin of Winter Root Vegetables

— • —

Steamed Fig Pudding

WORK PLAN

AT LEAST ONE DAY IN ADVANCE

Make the toast points and rinse
the watercress

Separate the leaves of the Brussels sprouts

Prepare the puff pastry rolls

THE DAY OF THE PARTY

Bake the puff pastry rolls

Make the eggnog

Cook the roast

Assemble the gratin

Make the steamed pudding and
whip the cream

Assemble the smoked salmon appetizer

JUST BEFORE SERVING

Cook the Brussels sprouts

Bake the gratin

Bake the Yorkshire pudding

Make the lobster salad

Napkins with Ornament Tie

Placing a hand-tied cloth napkin outfitted with an ornament at the center of each dinner plate adds a note of cheer and individuality to your holiday table décor. At the end of the meal, guests can take home their ornaments to hang on next year's Christmas tree.

lay a quartered napkin out flat. Bring together the two opposite corners, slightly folded back on themselves, and lay them one on top of the other.

tie each napkin around the center with a complementary satin ribbon in an overhand knot to hold the napkin's shape.

slip a glittering Christmas ornament onto the ribbon and finish the knot with a bow, leaving ample ends.

pour the prepared eggnog from a pitcher into cups or glasses set on a decorated tray.

whip the cream into soft peaks using an electric mixer and scoop into a serving bowl.

spoon a large dollop of the cream onto each serving of eggnog and sprinkle lightly with nutmeg and cinnamon.

Eggnog with Nutmeg and Cinnamon

Here, eggnog is topped with sweetened whipped cream and freshly ground spices.

1 or 2 whole nutmegs

1 cinnamon stick

12 large egg yolks

4 cups (32 fl oz/1 l) whole milk

1¼ cups (10 oz/310 g) sugar

2 cups (16 fl oz/500 ml) heavy (double) cream

½ teaspoon vanilla extract (essence)

1½ cups (12 fl oz/375 ml) brandy, Cognac, rum, or bourbon

Using a nutmeg grater or the smallest rasps on a handheld grater-shredder, grate the nutmeg until you have about 1 teaspoon. In a spice grinder or a coffee grinder reserved for spices, grind the cinnamon stick. Set aside.

In a large saucepan, whisk together the egg yolks, 2 cups (16 fl oz/500 ml) of the milk, and 1 cup (8 oz/250 g) of the sugar. Place over low heat and simmer, stirring often, until slightly thickened, 8–10 minutes. Remove from the heat, stir in the remaining 2 cups (16 fl oz/500 ml) milk, and let cool.

In a bowl, using a handheld mixer or whisk, whip the cream with the remaining ¼ cup (2 oz/60 g) sugar and the vanilla until soft peaks form. Set aside.

Strain the cooled mixture through a fine-mesh sieve and pour into a serving pitcher or a small punch bowl. Stir in the brandy. Serve the eggnog in cups or glasses, topped with a dollop of the whipped cream and a sprinkle each of nutmeg and cinnamon.

Serves 8–10

SMOKED SALMON AND WATERCRESS CREAM ON TOAST POINTS

Ideal for spreads, toast points are made by trimming the crusts from thin-sliced white bread, cutting the slices into triangles, and toasting them.

Preheat the oven to 350°F (180°C). Trim the crusts from the bread and discard. Cut each bread slice on the diagonal to make 4 triangles. Lay them on an ungreased baking sheet and bake until lightly golden, about 15 minutes. Turn and bake until the second side is lightly golden as well, about 10 minutes longer. Let cool.

In a bowl, mix together the crème fraîche, minced watercress, salt, and white pepper. Cut the smoked salmon into bite-sized pieces. Spread each toast with the crème fraîche mixture, top with a piece of salmon, and garnish with a watercress leaf. Arrange on a platter to serve.

8 thin slices white sandwich bread

1 cup (8 oz/250 g) crème fraîche

1 cup (1¹/₂ oz/45 g) minced watercress, plus whole leaves or sprigs for garnish

¹/₂ teaspoon salt

¹/₂ teaspoon freshly ground white pepper

3 oz (90 g) smoked salmon

ROQUEFORT AND WALNUT PUFF PASTRY ROLLS

Puff pastry is spread with a mixture of cheese and nuts and then rolled and cut into pinwheels. Freezing before baking will ensure a good puff.

Preheat the oven to 400°F (200°C). Line 2 baking sheets with parchment (baking) paper. Lay the puff pastry sheet on a lightly floured work surface and roll out ¹/₄ inch (6 mm) thick. Cut it in half lengthwise. In a bowl, using a fork, mix together the cheese with enough cream to make a spreadable paste. Spread half of the mixture on each half of the pastry to within ¹/₄ inch (6 mm) of the edges. Sprinkle evenly with the nuts and rosemary. Starting from a long side, roll up each pastry sheet and pinch the seam to seal. Using a sharp knife, cut the rolls crosswise into slices ¹/₂ inch (12 mm) thick. Arrange standing upright on the prepared baking sheets.

Freeze for 15 minutes, then transfer the cold baking sheets to the oven and bake until the pastry rolls are puffed and golden, 12–15 minutes. Let cool for 10 minutes before serving.

Each recipe serves 8–10

1 sheet puff pastry, about 11 by 14 inches (28 by 35 cm), thawed if frozen

3 oz (90 g) Roquefort cheese, at room temperature

2–4 tablespoons (1–2 fl oz/30–60 ml) heavy (double) cream

¹/₂ cup (2 oz/60 g) finely chopped walnuts

2 tablespoons minced fresh rosemary

LOBSTER SALAD WITH TARRAGON AND CHAMPAGNE VINAIGRETTE

You can use either whole lobsters or lobster tails to make this elegant salad. Serve it on a bed of fresh herbs, which makes for an attractive presentation and enhances the flavors of the salad. The herbs can be replaced with equal portions of field greens and baby arugula leaves.

1 tablespoon coarse sea salt or kosher salt

1¹/₂ lb (750 g) fresh lobster meat or 5 frozen lobster tails, thawed and halved lengthwise

2¹/₂ tablespoons Champagne vinegar

2 teaspoons fresh lemon juice

3¹/₂ tablespoons olive oil

¹/₂ teaspoon fine sea salt

¹/₂ teaspoon freshly ground pepper

2 teaspoons minced fresh tarragon

2–2¹/₂ cups (2–2¹/₂ oz/60–75 g) mixed delicate fresh herbs such as whole tarragon leaves, baby arugula (rocket) leaves, flat-leaf (Italian) parsley leaves, and watercress leaves, and small chervil sprigs

If using frozen lobster tails, bring a large pot three-fourths full of water to a boil over high heat. Add the coarse sea salt. Put the lobster tails in the pot and boil them until the shells are bright red and the meat is almost opaque throughout, about 8 minutes.

Meanwhile, ready a large bowl full of ice. When the lobster tails are done, transfer them immediately to the tub and cover with ice. (This quick cooling causes the flesh to pull away from the shell, making it easier to remove the meat.) Leave in the ice for 30 minutes. Remove the meat from the tails.

Whether using fresh or frozen, cut the lobster meat into generous bite-sized pieces. Set aside.

In a large bowl, combine 2 tablespoons of the vinegar, the fresh lemon juice, 2 tablespoons of the olive oil, the fine sea salt, the pepper, and the minced tarragon and mix well. Add the lobster meat and gently turn the pieces in the vinaigrette until well coated.

Divide the mixed herbs evenly among individual shallow bowls or salad plates. Place about ¹/₂ cup (3 oz/90 g) of the lobster salad atop each bed of herbs. Add the remaining 1¹/₂ tablespoon olive oil and ¹/₂ tablespoon vinegar to the bowl, mix well, and drizzle a little over each serving. Serve at once.

Serves 8–10

STANDING RIB ROAST WITH GARLIC-PEPPERCORN CRUST

Multicolored mixtures of peppercorns are sold in many markets, and they make a milder crust than black peppercorns alone do. When buying the roast, ask for a butcher's cut, with the bones separated but tied back on, which will add flavor during roasting and ease during carving. While the roast is resting, you can bake the Yorkshire Pudding (page 90).

In a mortar and using a pestle, crush the garlic and sea salt together to form a paste. Alternatively, crush together in a bowl with the bottom of a wooden spoon, or use a mini food processor. Add the peppercorns, thyme, paprika, and olive oil and mix to form a paste. Rub the paste all over the roast, coating it well. Cover loosely with aluminum foil and let stand at room temperature for 30 minutes.

Preheat the oven to 450°F (230°C).

Place the roast, bone side down, in a large roasting pan and roast for 30 minutes. Baste with the pan juices and reduce the oven temperature to 350°F (180°C). Continue to roast until an instant-read thermometer inserted into the thickest part of the meat (but not touching bone) registers 120°F (49°C) for rare, about 1 hour longer; or 125°–130°F (52°–54°C) for medium-rare, about 1¼ hours longer.

Transfer the roast to a carving board and tent loosely with aluminum foil. Let rest for 20–30 minutes before carving. While the roast is resting, skim off ¼ cup (2 fl oz/60 ml) of the fat from the pan and discard the rest. Combine the fat with some of the pan drippings and reserve to make the Yorkshire pudding (page 90).

If desired, make a sauce for the roast: Place the roasting pan with the remaining drippings on the stove top over medium-high heat and add the wine and up to 1 cup (8 fl oz/250 ml) water. Bring to a boil, stirring and scraping up any browned bits from the pan bottom. Cook until the sauce is thickened and reduced to about 1½ cups (12 fl oz/375 ml), 8–10 minutes. Strain through a fine-mesh sieve into a saucepan until ready to serve.

To serve, carve the roast into slices ¼–½ inch (6–12 mm) thick. Place the slices on a warmed platter and drizzle them with a little of the pan sauce. Serve at once.

Serves 8–10

4 cloves garlic, coarsely chopped

1½ tablespoons coarse sea salt

1 tablespoon freshly ground medium-coarse mixed peppercorns or black peppercorns

1 tablespoon fresh thyme leaves, minced

2 teaspoons paprika

2 teaspoons extra-virgin olive oil

1 butcher's-cut standing rib roast, 10–12 lb (5–6 kg), with 5 ribs

1 cup (8 fl oz/250 ml) Zinfandel, Merlot, or other dry red wine combined with ½ cup (4 fl oz/125 ml) Port (optional)

HERBED YORKSHIRE PUDDING

Here, fresh herbs give classic Yorkshire pudding an extra twist. This recipe makes individual servings in a muffin pan.

1/4 cup (2 fl oz/60 ml) reserved fat from the beef roasting pan (page 89)

1 cup (5 oz/155 g) all-purpose (plain) flour

1 1/2 teaspoons fine sea salt

1/2 cup (3/4 oz/20 g) *each* minced fresh flat-leaf (Italian) parsley and chives

4 large eggs

1 1/2 cups (12 fl oz/375 ml) whole milk

Preheat the oven to 400°F (200°C). In a small saucepan over medium-high heat, warm the reserved beef fat. In a bowl, whisk together the flour, salt, parsley, and chives. In another bowl, whisk together the eggs and the milk and then whisk in the flour mixture until blended.

Distribute the heated beef fat among the cups of a muffin pan, then pour in the batter all at once. Bake for 15 minutes. Reduce the oven temperature to 350°F (180°C) and continue to bake until the pudding is puffed and golden brown, about 15 minutes longer. Remove from the oven and, using a table knife, loosen the sides of each pudding to remove them from the pan. Serve at once with the rib roast while the puddings are still warm and puffed.

BRAISED BRUSSELS SPROUTS WITH SAGE BUTTER

The leaves of the Brussels sprouts are separated before steaming and sautéing, which gives the finished dish appealing height and texture.

2 lb (1 kg) Brussels sprouts

5 tablespoons (2 1/2 oz/75 g) unsalted butter

3 tablespoons olive oil

1/4 cup (1/3 oz/10 g) chopped fresh sage leaves

1 1/2 teaspoons salt

1 teaspoon freshly ground pepper

Cut the base off each sprout and peel away as many of the leaves as you can. Cut the tightly wrapped inner core lengthwise into quarters. Put the leaves and quarters in a bowl with water to cover. Using your hands, transfer the sprouts, dripping water, to a large sauté pan. Add 1 cup (8 fl oz/250 ml) water, bring to a boil over medium-high heat, cover, reduce the heat to low, and cook until tender when pierced with a fork, about 15 minutes. Drain and rinse under cold running water.

Wipe the pan dry and add the butter, olive oil, and sage. Cook over medium heat until the oil is infused with the sage, about 3 minutes. Do not brown the sage. Add the Brussels sprouts, salt, and pepper and sauté until the leaves glisten, about 10 minutes. Taste and adjust the seasoning. Serve hot.

Each recipe serves 8–10

CREAMY GRATIN OF WINTER ROOT VEGETABLES

Parsnips, rutabagas, and turnips are combined with potatoes, then coarsely mashed, topped with cheese, and gratinéed. The root vegetables add texture while enhancing the background flavor of the potatoes.

Preheat the oven to 350°F (180°C). Lightly butter a 12-inch (30-cm) flameproof gratin dish.

Peel the parsnips, rutabagas, turnip, and potatoes and cut into 1-inch (2.5-cm) cubes. Put the vegetables in a stockpot, add water to cover by 4–5 inches (10–13 cm), and add the coarse sea salt. Bring to a boil over high heat, reduce the heat to medium, and cook, uncovered, until the vegetables are easily pierced with the tines of a fork, about 25 minutes.

Drain the vegetables well and transfer to a large bowl. Sprinkle with the fine sea salt and pepper and turn several times.

In a saucepan over medium heat, combine the half-and-half, whole milk, and the 2 tablespoons butter and heat, stirring occasionally, just until tiny bubbles form along the edge of the pan.

Pour half of the milk mixture over the vegetables and mash coarsely with a potato masher. When the milk mixture has been absorbed, add the remaining milk mixture and 3 tablespoons of the parsley. Mash coarsely again until well blended. Spoon the mashed mixture into the prepared gratin dish, smoothing the surface. Sprinkle the cheeses on top. Cut the remaining 1 teaspoon butter into bits and dot the top.

Bake until bubbles begin to form along the edges and the top begins to turn golden, 15–20 minutes. Preheat the broiler (grill) and broil (grill) until the top is golden, 3–4 minutes. Remove from the broiler and sprinkle with the remaining 1 tablespoon parsley. Serve hot.

Serves 8–10

3 large parsnips

2 small rutabagas

1 medium turnip

3 Yukon gold potatoes

1 tablespoon coarse sea salt or kosher salt

2 teaspoons fine sea salt

1 teaspoon freshly ground pepper

1/2 cup (4 fl oz/125 ml) half-and-half (half cream)

1/2 cup (4 fl oz/125 ml) whole milk

2 tablespoons plus 1 teaspoon unsalted butter

4 tablespoons (1/3 oz/10 g) minced fresh flat-leaf (Italian) parsley

3 tablespoons grated Parmesan cheese

3 tablespoons finely shredded Gruyère cheese

Steamed Fig Pudding

Steamed puddings are a special holiday dessert in England and can vary in texture and taste. This version has the flavor of a rich bread pudding.

1¹/₂ cups (8 oz/250 g) dried figs, tough stem ends trimmed

¹/₂ cup (3 oz/90 g) dried currants

1 cup (4 oz/125 g) walnuts, toasted

8 slices white sandwich bread, crusts removed

1¹/₄ cups (6¹/₂ oz/200 g) all-purpose (plain) flour

7 tablespoons (3¹/₂ oz/105 g) unsalted butter, at room temperature

¹/₂ cup (3¹/₂ oz/105 g) firmly packed dark brown sugar

3 large eggs

1 cup (8 fl oz/250 ml) whole milk

1 teaspoon vanilla extract (essence)

Boiling water as needed

1¹/₂ cups (12 fl oz/375 ml) heavy (double) cream

¹/₄ cup (2 oz/60 g) granulated sugar

Preheat the oven to 300°F (150°C). Butter a 7-cup (1¹/₂-qt/1.5-l) pudding mold.

In a small saucepan over medium-high heat, combine the figs, currants, and 2 cups (16 fl oz/500 ml) water and bring to a boil. Reduce the heat to low and simmer, uncovered, until the figs are tender but still hold their shape, about 20 minutes. Remove from the heat and let stand in the cooking liquid. Meanwhile, place the toasted walnuts in a food processor and pulse to grind finely.

Tear the bread into pea-sized crumbs. In a large bowl, whisk together the bread crumbs, walnuts, and flour. Using a slotted spoon, transfer the figs and currants to another bowl. Reserve the cooking liquid. Halve 8–10 of the figs lengthwise and press them, cut side down, in a decorative pattern in the prepared mold. Coarsely chop the remaining figs; set aside.

In a bowl, using an electric mixer on medium-high speed, beat together the butter and brown sugar until fluffy. Add the eggs one at a time, beating well after each addition. Beat in the milk and vanilla. Stir in the currants and chopped figs. Fold half of the flour mixture into the egg mixture. Fold in the remaining flour mixture. Pour the batter into the mold and fasten the lid. Place the mold on a rack in a large pot and pour in boiling water to reach halfway up the sides of the mold. Bring to a boil over high heat, reduce the heat to medium-low, cover the pot, and boil for 2 hours, being careful not to let it boil over and replenishing the water as needed to maintain the original level. The pudding should slowly steam.

Remove the mold from the water and let stand for 15 minutes. Remove the lid, invert the mold onto a platter, and tap gently to release the pudding.

Using an electric mixer on medium speed, whip the cream until soft peaks form. Slowly add the granulated sugar while continuing to whip until stiff peaks form. At the same time, bring the reserved fig liquid to a boil over high heat and cook until reduced to ¹/₂ cup (4 fl oz/125 ml) syrup, about 5 minutes.

To serve, cut the pudding into 1-inch (2.5-cm) wedges, drizzle some syrup alongside, and top with the whipped cream.

Serves 8–10

SNOW COUNTRY BREAKFAST

Gather your guests around a festive breakfast table—the fragrance of fresh-brewed coffee and just-baked coffee cake hot from the oven swirling in the air—for a welcome beginning to a chilly winter day. Don't hesitate to ask everyone to help out in the kitchen. Some guests can start preparing the drinks and slicing the fruit, while others

cook the eggs and sausages. This hearty morning fare, with its varied flavors, will provide everyone with ample energy for outdoor activities the remainder of the day.

MENU

Sparkling Citrus Spritzers

— • —

*Dried Apricot and Cranberry
Coffee Cake*

Shirred Eggs with Smoked Salmon

Baked Breakfast Sausages

Grilled Toast

Broiled Grapefruit with Brown Sugar

TIPS FOR A WINTER COUNTRY BREAKFAST

- For a bright and cheerful table, opt for a strong palette in a single color, including the dishes, linens, and table decorations.

- Bring nature indoors by incorporating seasonal blooms such as forced narcissus and gathered rosehips, pine cones, or chestnuts.

- Have hot, fresh coffee and tea ready for guests when they arrive.

- If children are present, serve them hot chocolate topped with whipped cream.

- If you have a fireplace, set a glowing fire for a warm welcome.

WORK PLAN

AT LEAST ONE DAY IN ADVANCE
Juice the citrus

THE MORNING OF THE BREAKFAST
Bake the coffee cake

JUST BEFORE SERVING
Make the spritzers

Broil the grapefruit

Grill the toast

Bake the sausages

Cook the eggs

ROSEHIP AND NARCISSUS CENTERPIECE

A floral centerpiece designed especially for the breakfast table makes the morning meal a special occasion. Creating this striking arrangement is easy using readily purchased plants and materials.

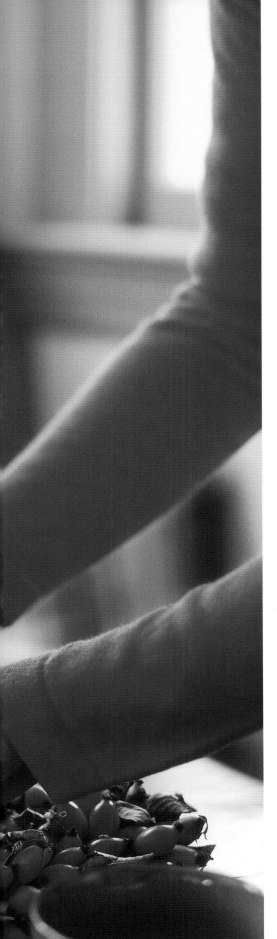

gather everything you'll need: potted narcissus, neutral-colored planters, square or round rosehip wreaths to match the shape of the planters, and sphagnum moss.

lay the rosehip wreaths down the center of the table, spacing them evenly among the place settings.

place the potted bulbs in the planters and tuck the moss loosely around the base of the bulbs, so it appears the flowers are growing out of the moss.

nestle a planter of bulbs in the center of each wreath, adjusting placement as necessary to keep sight lines clear.

squeeze the orange and grapefruit juices the night before. Mix them together, then stir in the lime juice just before serving.

fill each glass with ice cubes and the mixed juices, then top off with sparkling water.

garnish each glass with a colorful piece of fruit, such as thin slices of citrus speared on a toothpick.

SPARKLING CITRUS SPRITZERS

These breakfast spritzers, made with a mixture of grapefruit and orange juices, get an extra burst of flavor from a sprinkling of lime juice just before sparkling mineral water is added.

2 cups (16 fl oz/500 ml) fresh
grapefruit juice

2 cups (16 fl oz/500 ml) fresh
orange juice

12–18 ice cubes

1/4 cup (2 fl oz/60 ml) fresh lime juice

4 cups (32 fl oz/1 l) sparkling mineral
water, chilled

Citrus slices for garnish, quartered

Sugar

In a large pitcher, combine the grapefruit and orange juices. Add 2 or 3 ice cubes to each of 6 tall glasses. Stir the lime juice into the juice mixture and divide evenly among the glasses. Fill the glasses with the sparkling mineral water and garnish with citrus slices. Let guests add sugar to taste.

Serves 6

DRIED APRICOT AND CRANBERRY COFFEE CAKE

Here, scatter dried fruits on top of a light cake batter, then sprinkle them with a sugar crumble mix, to create a sweet, melted topping that keeps the fruits moist. Serve the coffee cake warm.

Preheat the oven to 400°F (200°C). Lightly butter an 8-inch (20-cm) square baking pan and set aside.

In a bowl, whisk together the 1¹/₂ cups flour, ¹/₂ cup (4 oz/125 g) of the sugar, the baking powder, and the cinnamon. In another bowl, whisk together the egg, milk, and the melted butter. Pour the egg mixture into the dry ingredients and mix well. Pour the batter into the prepared pan and spread evenly.

In a small bowl, combine the remaining ¹/₂ cup sugar, 3 tablespoons flour, and 2 tablespoons cold butter. Using your fingertips, work the ingredients together to make a coarse crumble. Sprinkle the dried fruits over the batter, and then sprinkle with the crumble mixture.

Bake until a toothpick inserted into the center comes out clean, about 30 minutes. Let cool on a wire rack for 15–30 minutes before serving. To serve, cut into squares.

Serves 6

1¹/₂ cups (7¹/₂ oz/235 g) plus
3 tablespoons all-purpose (plain) flour

1 cup (8 oz/250 g) sugar

2¹/₄ teaspoons baking powder

¹/₂ teaspoon ground cinnamon

1 large egg

¹/₂ cup (4 fl oz/125 ml) whole milk

4 tablespoons (2 oz/60 g) unsalted
butter, melted, plus 2 tablespoons
cold butter

¹/₄ cup (1¹/₂ oz/45 g) chopped dried
apricots or dried peaches

¹/₄ cup (1 oz/30 g) chopped dried
cranberries

SHIRRED EGGS WITH SMOKED SALMON

Small, soft curds form as eggs are gently cooked and stirred in the top of a double boiler set over simmering water. Add slivers of salmon and a scattering of minced chives just before removing the creamy eggs from the heat, then serve.

12 large eggs

7 tablespoons (3¹/₂ oz/105 g) unsalted butter, cut into ¹/₂-inch (12-mm) pieces

2 teaspoons freshly ground pepper

3 oz (90 g) smoked salmon, cut into slivers ¹/₄ inch (6 mm) wide

2 tablespoons minced fresh chives

Salt (optional)

In the bottom pan of a large double boiler, bring enough water to reach just below the top pan almost to a boil. (Alternatively, use a large saucepan and a large metal bowl.) In a bowl, lightly whisk the eggs. Stir in the butter pieces and pepper and pour the egg mixture into the top pan of the double boiler. Whisk the eggs continuously until they start to thicken, about 10 minutes. Add the salmon and chives and continue to whisk until a creamy mass of tiny curds has formed, 1–2 minutes longer. The curds should be soft, not firm. Taste and add salt if desired. Transfer to a warmed platter and serve hot.

Serves 6

BAKED BREAKFAST SAUSAGES

Baked sausages feed a crowd with minimum effort. To ensure they cook evenly, elevate them on the rack of a broiler pan, and allow any excess fat to drip down into the pan, or outfit a roasting pan or baking pan with a rack.

18–24 breakfast sausage links, 1¹/₂–2 lb (750 g–1 kg) total weight

Preheat the oven to 400°F (200°C).

Place the sausages on a rack in a shallow roasting pan or broiler (grill) pan. Roast until the sausages are shiny but not yet browned, about 10 minutes. Turn the sausages and continue roasting until cooked through, about 5 minutes longer.

Preheat the broiler. Place the pan under the broiler and broil (grill) just long enough to brown the sausages, 2–3 minutes on each side. Transfer to a warmed platter and serve hot.

Serves 6

GRILLED TOAST

The perfect accompaniment for shirred eggs, grilled toast is easy to prepare for a group of guests on a winter's morning.

Preheat the broiler (grill) and adjust the rack so it is about 4 inches (10 cm) from the heat source. In a small saucepan over medium heat, melt the butter. Brush each bread slice on both sides with the melted butter.

Place the bread slices directly on the rack and broil (grill) until golden brown, 2–3 minutes on each side. Remove from the broiler and serve at once.

Serves 6

2 tablespoons unsalted butter

About 12 slices brioche

BROILED GRAPEFRUIT WITH BROWN SUGAR

Just enough brown sugar is sprinkled over freshly cut grapefruit halves to melt and caramelize slightly under the broiler. Use either pink or white grapefruit, depending on availability and your preference. If you wish, section the grapefruit before broiling to make it easier to eat.

3 grapefruits, halved

6 tablespoons (3 oz/90 g) firmly packed light brown sugar

Preheat the broiler (grill) and adjust the rack so it is about 4 inches (10 cm) from the heat source.

Arrange the grapefruit halves, cut side up, on a broiler pan. Sprinkle each half with 1 tablespoon of the brown sugar. Broil (grill) until the sugar is melted and starting to bubble, 2–3 minutes. Remove from the broiler and serve at once.

Serves 6

NEW YEAR'S DAY OPEN HOUSE

After the bustle of Christmas, an easygoing buffet is a relaxed way to welcome the New Year. Set the table and arrange the coffee service area early in the day or even the night before to keep everything running smoothly once the guests begin to arrive. Lay a festive fabric runner the length of the table, put the cutlery in a colorful jar or

bowl, and place rolled napkins and a stack of earth-toned plates alongside. A simple seasonal centerpiece of sprays of rosehips or branches of witch hazel adds color to the scene. The menu, composed of robust flavors and hearty fare, will warm guests on this winter holiday.

TIPS FOR AN OPEN HOUSE

- Set up a buffet table at least 4 feet (1.3 m) from any wall so that guests can reach it from all sides, or place it in the center of the room.

- Arrange different areas where guests can sit and eat comfortably.

- To keep the flow of guests smooth, designate a separate service area for drinks and another area for desserts.

- Place appetizers on a coffee table, rather than the buffet table, to distinguish the parts of the meal.

MENU

Hot Spiced Red Wine

Rosemary Roasted Almonds

Goat Cheese and Shallot Toasts

— • —

White Bean Soup with Escarole

Field Greens with Homemade Croutons

— • —

Bourbon-Glazed Ham

Roasted Potatoes with Sea Salt

Broccoli and Blue Cheese Gratin

Apple and Fennel Slaw

— • —

Gingerbread with Whipped Cream

WORK PLAN

AT LEAST ONE DAY IN ADVANCE

Mix the cheese spread and toast
the bread

Roast the almonds

Make the croutons

Make the slaw

THE DAY OF THE PARTY

Prepare the wine

Assemble the toasts

Make the soup

Bake the ham

Cook the broccoli and make the sauce

Bake the gingerbread

JUST BEFORE SERVING

Bake the gratin

Cook the potatoes

Make the salad

Whip the cream

HOT SPICED RED WINE

With spices and sugar, hot spiced red wine makes a welcoming holiday drink for guests. This recipe features cinnamon, cloves, star anise, and vanilla, as well as thick slices of fragrant orange zest.

Remove the zest from the oranges in strips about $^1/_2$ inch (12 mm) wide. Set aside 2 long strips. Cut the remaining strips into 6–8 pieces each $1^1/_2$–2 inches (4–5 cm) long, then cut a small slit in each so that the zest can be slipped onto the rim of a glass as a garnish.

In a nonreactive saucepan, combine the wine, the 2 long orange zest strips, the cinnamon sticks, cloves, star anise, vanilla bean pieces, and sugar. Place over medium-high heat and bring almost to a boil, stirring to dissolve the sugar. Reduce the heat to low and simmer for 5 minutes.

Serve from the stove or pour the red wine mixture into a small punch bowl and ladle servings into heat-resistant glasses. Slip a piece of zest on the rim of each glass.

Serves 12–14

Strips of zest from 2 oranges

2 bottles (48 fl oz/1.5 l) Syrah or Merlot

2 cinnamon sticks, about 4 inches (10 cm) long

8 whole cloves

2 star anise pods

2 pieces vanilla bean, about 2 inches (5 cm) long

$^1/_2$ cup (4 oz/125 g) sugar

HOT-BEVERAGE SLEEVES

When serving hot drinks at a buffet, glasses should be outfitted with heat-resistant sleeves so they will be comfortable for guests to carry. Sleeves might be made of woven straw, felt, or even a napkin tied attractively around each glass.

arrange glasses, sleeves, and garnishes together on a tray next to the hot wine.

slip each glass into one of the heat-resistant sleeves. Ladle the hot beverage carefully into the glasses.

garnish each glass with a strip of orange zest before passing it to a guest.

ROSEMARY ROASTED ALMONDS

For a less pronounced rosemary flavor, omit the minced rosemary and use only the sprigs. If desired, more sea salt can be added just before serving the almonds.

Preheat the oven to 350°F (180°C). Have ready an ungreased baking sheet.

In a bowl, combine the almonds, olive oil, salt, pepper, minced rosemary, and rosemary sprigs. Turn to coat the almonds well. Mound the mixture on the baking sheet. Roast, turning a few times, until the almonds are beginning to lightly brown, 20–25 minutes. Transfer the almonds to paper towels and let cool. Discard the rosemary sprigs. Transfer the cooled almonds to an airtight container lined with waxed paper and store in a cool, dry place for up to 2 weeks.

Serves 12–14

2 1/4 cups (12 oz/375 g) whole unblanched almonds

3 tablespoons extra-virgin olive oil

1 tablespoon sea salt

1 teaspoon freshly ground pepper

3 tablespoons minced fresh rosemary

4 fresh rosemary sprigs, each 6 inches (15 cm) long

GOAT CHEESE AND SHALLOT TOASTS

The addition of sweet cream to soft goat cheese tempers its tanginess while making it light and easy to spread. Pink peppercorns scattered across the top add color and complement the shallots.

Preheat the oven to 350°F (180°C). Have ready 2 ungreased baking sheets.

Cut the baguette on the diagonal into slices 1/4 inch (6 mm) thick. Arrange the slices in a single layer on the baking sheets. Bake until lightly golden, about 15 minutes. Turn the slices and bake until the second side is lightly golden as well, about 10 minutes longer. Set aside.

Put the goat cheese in a bowl and mash it with a fork. Add 1 tablespoon of the cream and mash it in. Continue to add the cream, 1 tablespoon at a time, until you have a soft, mild spread. Mix in the salt and the shallots to taste.

When ready to serve, spread each baguette toast with the cheese and shallot spread and top with several pink peppercorns.

Serves 12–14

1 baguette

5 oz (155 g) soft goat cheese, at room temperature

4–6 tablespoons (2–3 fl oz/60–90 ml) heavy (double) cream

1/2 teaspoon salt

2 or 3 small shallots, minced

3 tablespoons pink peppercorns, smashed

White Bean Soup with Escarole

This uncomplicated soup, full of the simple flavors of beans, broth, and greens, can be enjoyed by the cup or bowl. Offer guests freshly grated Parmesan cheese to sprinkle over the top.

2¼ cups (16 oz/500 g) dried cannellini, white kidney, flageolet, or small lima beans

1 tablespoon plus 1 teaspoon coarse sea salt or kosher salt

1½ heads escarole (Batavian endive)

3 tablespoons extra-virgin olive oil

1½ small yellow onions, minced

8 cups (64 fl oz/2 l) chicken stock or reduced-sodium chicken broth

1 teaspoon freshly ground pepper

2 bay leaves

¾ cup (3 oz/90 g) grated Parmesan cheese

Pour 8 qt (8 l) water into a large pot, add the beans and the 1 tablespoon salt, then bring to a boil over medium-high heat. Reduce the heat to low, cover partially, and simmer until the beans are tender to the bite, 2–2½ hours. Using a slotted spoon, transfer the beans to a bowl and set aside, reserving the cooking liquid in the pot. You should have about 8 cups (64 fl oz/2 l) liquid remaining. Return the bean broth to a gentle boil over medium-high heat and cook until reduced to about 4 cups (32 fl oz/1 l), about 10 minutes.

Hold the escarole to make a tight bunch. Using a sharp knife, cut the escarole crosswise into strips ¼ inch (6 mm) wide, then chop coarsely. Set aside.

In a clean pot over medium heat, warm the olive oil. When the oil is hot, add the onions and sauté until translucent, 3–4 minutes. Add the escarole and cook, stirring, until it wilts, 2–3 minutes. Add the chicken stock, the reduced bean cooking liquid, the pepper, the 1 teaspoon salt, and the bay leaves. Raise the heat to high and bring to a boil. Reduce the heat to low and simmer, uncovered, until the flavors are blended, about 30 minutes. Stir in the beans and cook for 5 minutes longer.

Taste and adjust the seasoning. Serve hot, garnished with the Parmesan cheese.

Serves 12–14

FIELD GREENS WITH HOMEMADE CROUTONS

These croutons, made by browning cubes cut from a day-old baguette in garlic-flavored oil and seasoning them with sea salt and thyme, can be made a day in advance and added to the salad just before serving. Make an extra batch; they always prove popular, especially with children.

Cut the bread slices into 1-inch (2.5-cm) cubes. In a frying pan over medium heat, warm $^1/_3$ cup (3 fl oz/80 ml) of the olive oil. Add the garlic, reduce the heat to low, and sauté until golden, 2–3 minutes, being careful not to let it burn. Using a slotted spoon, remove the garlic and discard.

Add the bread cubes to the garlic oil and return the pan to low heat. Sauté slowly, turning once, until golden and crusty, 4–5 minutes on each side. Sprinkle with the fine sea salt and the thyme, toss briefly, and transfer the croutons to paper towels to drain. Let cool.

In a large serving bowl, combine the mustard and the remaining $^2/_3$ cup (5 fl oz/ 170 ml) olive oil and mix together with a fork until thickened, about 2 minutes. Mix in the red wine vinegar, balsamic vinegar, coarse sea salt, and pepper.

Just before serving, add the field greens and toss well to coat generously with the vinaigrette. Add half of the croutons and toss again to coat. Garnish the salad with the remaining croutons.

Serves 12–14

12 slices day-old baguette, each 1 inch (2.5 cm) thick

1 cup (8 fl oz/250 ml) extra-virgin olive oil

2 cloves garlic, crushed

$^3/_4$ teaspoon fine sea salt

1 tablespoon minced fresh thyme

1 tablespoon Dijon mustard

$^1/_3$ cup (3 fl oz/80 ml) red wine vinegar

$1^1/_2$ tablespoons balsamic vinegar

$1^1/_2$ teaspoons coarse sea salt

$1^1/_2$ teaspoons freshly ground pepper

2 lb (1 kg) mixed young field greens or a mixture of field greens and baby spinach

Bourbon-Glazed Ham

A whole ham, glistening with a sugary glaze, forms a striking centerpiece. Slice the ham thin or thick or cook a spiral-cut ham, equally flavorful.

1 fully cooked, bone-in whole ham, about 20 lb (10 kg)

2 1/2 cups (17 1/2 oz/545 g) firmly packed dark brown sugar

1/3 cup (3 fl oz/80 ml) bourbon

15–20 whole cloves

Preheat the oven to 325°F (165°C). Line a shallow roasting pan with aluminum foil and set a roasting rack in the pan. Cut away and discard any skin from the ham and trim the fat to 1/2 inch (12 mm) thick. Place the ham, fat side up, on the rack in the roasting pan. Roast until the ham is fully warmed through and an instant-read thermometer inserted into the thickest part of the ham (but not touching bone) registers 140°F (60°C), 3–3 1/2 hours.

Remove the ham from the oven. Raise the oven temperature to 425°F (220°C). In a bowl, combine the brown sugar and bourbon and mix to make a paste. Score the fat on the upper half of the ham in a diamond pattern, cutting about 1/4 inch (6 mm) deep. Rub the paste over the surface, then place the cloves at random intersections of the diamonds. Return the ham to the oven and bake, basting several times with the pan juices, until the surface is shiny and beginning to brown, 15–20 minutes.

Transfer the ham to a cutting board and tent loosely with aluminum foil. Let stand for 20–30 minutes. Remove the cloves. Carve half of the ham and arrange on a warmed platter. Carve the remaining ham as needed.

Serves 12–14, with leftovers

Roasted Potatoes with Sea Salt

Long, slow roasting in olive oil with a sea salt rub produces potatoes with a slightly crunchy skin and a creamy interior.

42–48 baby red potatoes, about 6 lb (3 kg) total weight, each 1 1/2–2 inches (4–5 cm) in diameter

1/3 cup (3 fl oz/80 ml) extra-virgin olive oil

1 1/2 tablespoons coarse sea salt

15–20 large fresh sage sprigs

Preheat the oven to 350°F (180°C). Arrange the potatoes in a single layer in a large roasting pan. Pour the oil over them and turn to coat well. Sprinkle with the salt, turn again, and tuck in the sage sprigs. Roast until the skins are slightly wrinkled and the interior is tender and creamy when pierced with the tip of a sharp knife, about 1 1/2 hours.

Serves 12–14

Broccoli and Blue Cheese Gratin

Choose a more mild blue cheese, such as Bleu d'Auvergne or Gorgonzola, for this recipe. Broccoli is first steamed until tender and then cloaked with cheese sauce and topped with buttery crumbs for baking.

Preheat the oven to 350°F (180°C). Lightly butter a 12-inch (30-cm) gratin dish.

Trim and discard the thick stalks from the broccoli. Cut the heads in half lengthwise. Place the broccoli in a steamer rack set over boiling water. Cover and steam until easily pierced with the tines of a fork, about 15 minutes. Drain and rinse under cold running water, then coarsely chop. Drain again, transfer to a bowl, and set aside.

In a frying pan over medium heat, melt 1 tablespoon of the butter. Add the bread crumbs and cook, stirring, until golden brown, about 5 minutes. Remove from the heat and set aside.

In a saucepan over medium-high heat, melt 4½ tablespoons (2¼ oz/67 g) of the butter. When the butter has melted, remove the pan from the heat and whisk in the flour to make a roux. Return the pan to low heat and slowly pour in 1 cup (8 fl oz/250 ml) of the milk, whisking constantly. Reduce the heat to low and simmer, stirring occasionally, until thickened, 7–10 minutes. Whisk in another 1 cup milk. Add the salt, black pepper, and cayenne pepper. Continue to simmer, stirring occasionally, until the mixture has thickened again, 5–7 minutes. Whisk in the remaining 1 cup milk and simmer until thick enough to coat the back of a spoon, about 5 minutes longer. Stir in the blue cheese and cook, stirring, just until melted, about 2 minutes. Remove from the heat.

Pour the sauce over the broccoli and turn gently to mix. Spoon the mixture into the prepared gratin dish, smooth the surface, and top with the buttered bread crumbs. Cut the remaining 1 tablespoon butter into bits and dot the top. Bake until bubbling around the edges and golden on top, about 20 minutes. Serve hot or warm.

Serves 12–14

6 large heads broccoli, about 4½ lb (2.25 kg) total weight

6½ tablespoons (3¼ oz/97 g) unsalted butter

¾ cup (1½ oz/45 g) fresh bread crumbs

4½ tablespoons (1½ oz/45 g) all-purpose (plain) flour

3 cups (24 fl oz/750 ml) whole milk

1 teaspoon fine sea salt

1 teaspoon freshly ground black pepper

⅛ teaspoon cayenne pepper

3 oz (90 g) blue cheese, crumbled

APPLE AND FENNEL SLAW

Chilling the apples, fennel, and cabbage in ice water before dressing keeps them crunchy and helps to retain their individual flavors. The fennel is blanched to tenderize it and chilled again for crunch. Golden raisins complement the tart, sweet dressing.

1 head green cabbage

Ice water as needed

1 lemon, halved

4 fennel bulbs

4 Granny Smith apples

1 cup (8 fl oz/250 ml) mayonnaise

1/4 cup (2 oz/60 g) sugar

1/4 cup (2 fl oz/60 ml) fresh lemon juice

1/4 cup (2 fl oz/60 ml) sherry vinegar

2 tablespoons whole milk, or more if needed

1 teaspoon salt

1 cup (6 oz/185 g) golden raisins (sultanas)

4 green (spring) onions, including tender green parts, thinly sliced

1/2 cup (3/4 oz/20 g) minced fresh flat-leaf (Italian) parsley

Using a sharp knife, cut the cabbage in half through the stem end. Slice the cut face of each half into paper-thin slices. Place the sliced cabbage in a large bowl and add ice water to cover. Set aside.

Fill another large bowl with ice water and squeeze the juice of 1/2 lemon into it. Bring a large saucepan three-fourths full of water to a boil over high heat and add the juice of the remaining lemon half. Cut off the stems and feathery fronds of the fennel bulbs and remove any bruised or discolored outer leaves. Working with 1 fennel bulb at a time, cut the bulb in half lengthwise and cut out any tough core parts. Using the small julienne blade of a mandoline, slice each half into matchsticks and place immediately in the bowl of lemon water. Repeat with the remaining fennel bulbs. When all the fennel is cut, transfer with a slotted spoon to the boiling water and blanch for 30 seconds. (Reserve the bowl of water and lemon for the apples.) Drain the blanched fennel and rinse well under cold running water. Transfer to a fresh bowl of ice water. Set aside.

Working with 1 apple at a time, quarter it and cut away the core. Starting with the rounded side, slice each quarter into matchsticks on the mandoline and place immediately in the reserved lemon water. Repeat with the remaining apples.

In another bowl, combine the mayonnaise, sugar, lemon juice, vinegar, milk, and the salt and mix together. Taste. The dressing should be both sweet and tangy, and the consistency should be pourable, not thick. Add a little more milk if the dressing is too thick. Taste and adjust the seasoning.

Drain the cabbage, pat dry, and place in a large bowl. Drain the fennel, squeeze gently to remove excess water, pat dry, and add to the bowl of cabbage. Drain the apples, pat dry, and add to the bowl. Add the raisins, green onions, and parsley. Pour the dressing over all and mix well. Cover and refrigerate until ready to serve.

Serves 12–14

GINGERBREAD WITH WHIPPED CREAM

Ginger in three forms triples the impact of this cake. You can top each slice with a dollop of whipped cream and a sprinkle of crystallized ginger, or you can frost the cake with the cream just before serving and scatter the ginger evenly over the top.

Preheat the oven to 350°F (180°C). Line a 12-by-17-inch (30-by-43-cm) half-sheet pan or two 7-by-11-by-1¹/₂-inch (18-by-28-by-4-cm) baking pans with parchment (baking) paper.

In a bowl, whisk together the flour, baking soda, salt, ground ginger, cinnamon, and allspice. In a large bowl, using an electric mixer on medium-high speed, beat the butter and brown sugar together until creamy. Beat in the egg. Add the molasses and freshly grated ginger and beat until well mixed, about 2 minutes. Beat in the flour mixture in 3 batches, alternating with the buttermilk in 2 batches. Using a rubber spatula, scrape the batter evenly into the prepared pan(s).

Bake until a toothpick inserted in the center comes out clean, 25–30 minutes. Let cool in the pan on a wire rack for 10 minutes. Slip an icing spatula between the paper and the pan(s) and then gently invert the cake(s) onto the rack. (If making a large single sheet of gingerbread, place 2 or 3 racks together.) Peel off the paper, turn the cake(s) right side up, and let cool completely on the rack(s). Transfer the cooled cake(s) to a cutting board. Set aside until ready to serve.

Using the electric mixer on medium-high speed, beat the cream. Sprinkle in all of the confectioners' sugar and beat until soft peaks form. Cover and refrigerate until ready to serve the cake. Briefly beat the cream again with a whisk if there is any separation.

Cut the cake into triangles and arrange the triangles on a platter or pedestal. Top each serving with a dollop of whipped cream. Scatter the crystallized ginger over the cream and serve.

Serves 12–14

3 cups (15 oz/470 g) all-purpose (plain) flour

1 teaspoon baking soda (bicarbonate of soda)

¹/₂ teaspoon salt

1 tablespoon ground ginger

1 teaspoon ground cinnamon

1 teaspoon ground allspice

1 cup (8 oz/250 g) unsalted butter, at room temperature

1 cup (7 oz/220 g) firmly packed light brown sugar

1 large egg

1 cup (11 oz/345 g) light molasses

¹/₄ cup (1¹/₂ oz/45 g) peeled and grated fresh ginger

1 cup (8 fl oz/250 ml) buttermilk

1¹/₂ cups (12 fl oz/375 ml) heavy (double) cream

6 tablespoons (1¹/₂ oz/45 g) confectioners' (icing) sugar

³/₄ cup (4¹/₂ oz/140 g) minced crystallized ginger

TRANSFORMING YOUR HOME FOR THE HOLIDAYS

The pleasures of holiday entertaining, whether you are hosting a big Christmas dinner or having only a few friends over for cocktails, will be greatly enhanced if you take time earlier in the month to get the house ready. Cleaning, decorating, hanging lights, and trimming the tree will put you in a holiday mood and make your home warm and inviting for guests all through the season, no matter what kind of entertaining you do.

Natural Decorations

The most delightful holiday decorations are often the simplest and most natural. Rather than buy expensive baubles, plan a trip to a local flower or farmers' market or floral-supply store to buy boughs, garlands, and wreaths of pine, cedar, spruce, olive, eucalyptus, holly, and other greenery that will remain vibrant for several weeks. You can supplement these with greenery from your own garden. Stock up on floral wire and tape, along with pine cones, sprays of bright berries, seasonal produce, and other natural decorative items.

Lay everything out in an uncluttered workspace, and let the shapes and colors of the greenery be your guide as you use it to decorate the entryway, mantel, family room, dining room, and kitchen. To give the house a unified feeling, choose a simple palette of just two or three colors, such as red, white, or green with accents of gold or silver. You might want to use similar colors when decorating the Christmas tree.

Use ribbon to enhance greenery and to secure it in place. Tying a spray of pine to a rustic chandelier, a candelabra, or a banister is an easy way to transform an everyday element into a festive one. Snow-white cut flowers, such as roses, miniature calla lilies, or tulips set in glass vases make stunning wintertime arrangements. Or use forced bulbs of crocus, hyacinth, paperwhite narcissus, or amaryllis in terra-cotta pots or glass bowls to create a cheery and seasonal white-and-green look.

Lighting

Incorporate candles into your decorations to add warmth and sparkle. These can be simple off-white pillars in varying heights and shapes, votives in clear or colored glasses, or elegant tapers. Or, choose candles in one or more colors that coordinate with your holiday palette. In every case, however, select dripless candles to avoid damaging

tabletops or other surfaces and to eliminate the need for post-party cleanup. Lower or turn off overhead lighting when possible to let the twinkling candles, the glow of the tree, and the light of the fire create a magical effect. Hurricane lamps, oil lamps, and luminarias (votives anchored in sand inside paper bags) work well for both indoor and outdoor decorating. Remember, lighting the way to your front door helps set the tone of a warm welcome to your guests.

Seasonal Scents and Sounds

Keep apple cider or red wine and cinnamon sticks and whole cloves on hand so you can prepare a batch of hot cider or mulled wine when guests show up. As it heats, it will fill your home with the welcoming aroma of holiday spices. You might also light some scented candles at this time of year. Stores typically stock seasonal scents, such as pine, cinnamon, and vanilla. They are especially nice placed near the front door or fire place. Keep the candles well away from the dining

area, however, so that the scents do not compete with the food.

Gather your holiday music recordings—maybe buy more, too—and, if you have a piano, set out some Christmas sheet music to encourage a spontaneous sing-along.

Decorative Table Elements

The best decorating tip for the holiday table is to avoid overdecorating. Start with a handful of beautiful elements in no more than a few colors. You can use virtually anything, from silver candlesticks or matching decanters to small, beautifully wrapped gifts, as long as the overall look remains focused, clean, and harmonious.

For the centerpiece, select complementary natural and decorative items that fit the mood of the holiday, such as fresh flowers and seasonal fruits, evergreen branches, ribbons, and Christmas ornaments. The fruits might be a colorful assortment of oranges and lemons, persimmons and crab apples, or perhaps pomegranates paired with a

handful of pecans and walnuts in their shells. If you decide on flowers, avoid any with a strong fragrance that will rival the aromas of your food. Arrange a few of these elements on a tray or platter, adding more in small batches until you have achieved a balance of colors and textures.

For a more casual look, create your arrangement directly on the surface of the table. Avoid tall elements that might block sight lines. Or, create an even simpler centerpiece, such as a wreath laid directly on the table with candles nestled inside it, a bowlful of ornaments, or a pitcher brimming with a single kind of flower. Aim to achieve an uncomplicated effect that relates to the other holiday decorations in the room.

You can add a matching decorative accent to each place setting, such as a small wrapped gift or ornament with a card that doubles as a place card, or a copy of the menu printed on pretty paper, rolled, and secured with a ribbon. Finally, select candles that will complement your holiday table.

ELEMENTS OF THE TABLE

Once you've decorated the house and the tree, the table comes next. Start with a few elements you know you would like to use—the good silverware, a special set of dishes, a favorite linen tablecloth and napkins—and design your table setting to match the mood those items inspire.

Dinnerware

The plates and serving dishes you choose can help set the overall tone for your celebration. Don't be concerned about all the pieces matching. What is important is that everything has a harmonious style and palette. Basic white plates are always a good choice for holiday entertaining because they work well in both elegant and casual settings and highlight the food. Augment them with solid-colored or lightly patterned serving dishes to create a contemporary or classic mood depending on your preference.

For a casual breakfast or lunch, use bright dishes paired with simple glassware, cotton linens, and silverware with clean lines. Once you have chosen serving platters and bowls, think about garnishes that add a splash of complementary holiday color, such as a scattering of green chives or a spray of red berries on a silver tray.

Glassware

Glassware brings shimmering richness to the holiday table. Classic stemware works well for either a formal or a casual meal. Setting the table with wineglasses and matching, larger water glasses is a good way to create a celebratory look. The glassware on a holiday table should sparkle, whether it is delicate crystal, fine stemware, or sturdy tumblers. As long as it is spotless and free of scratches, even an inexpensive set of glasses can bring a table setting together, simply because their matching shapes and sizes create a pleasing continuous pattern. For special beverages, tall, slender cocktail glasses, tumblers with a graceful contemporary line, or stemless wineglasses give even the simplest of holiday breakfast drinks, aperitifs, and cocktails an especially festive presentation.

Flatware

Christmas dinner is a perfect occasion to polish up the family silver or set out the good stainless and let its gleam enliven the table. If you have an eclectic collection of vintage flatware, mixing and matching from one place setting to the next can add character. Heavy restaurant-style flatware with thick handles and a no-nonsense, subtle design goes with virtually any place setting, contemporary or traditional.

Linens

For Christmas, a high-quality cotton or linen tablecloth is an excellent choice. Make sure your napkins are of similar quality, although they do not need to match the tablecloth. In fact, contrasting napkins can help tie the overall color scheme together. Add color or whimsy to each place setting by folding or tying the napkin with a decorative element, such as an ornament or holly sprig. Cloth napkin squares add an elegant touch to a cocktail party. For more casual settings, be creative with a variety of napkins that fit your overall palette, perhaps alternating colors at every other setting.

Setting the Holiday Table

A comfortable table setting, especially a formal one with extra glassware and flatware, should allow about two feet (60 cm) of space between the center of one plate and the center of the next.

The Informal Table

For casual Christmastime entertaining, consider setting the table without a cloth, or select a simple tablecloth or placemats in a neutral color and complementary napkins. A colorful runner, laid lengthwise down the center of the table, is an easy way to add holiday cheer. You can use everyday plates, flatware, and glassware, supplemented with a few special pieces. Set the napkin to the left of the plate, fold facing inward. Arrange flatware in the order in which it will be used, starting with the outermost item. Place the forks to the left of the plate and position the knife to the right, with its blade facing inward. Put the soupspoon to the right of the knife. Set a water glass above the knife and a wineglass to its right.

The Formal Table

At a formal table, guests always have a plate in front of them. A charger, or large plate, is set at each place, and the first course is served on a small plate set atop the charger. The charger is replaced with a dinner plate when the main course is served.

Place the napkin to the left of the plate, fold facing inward, with room for silverware to its right, or put the napkin on the plate. Silverware is seldom placed directly on the napkin, as it inhibits a guest's ability to pick it up easily. To the right of the napkin, place the forks in the order in which they will be used, from left to right. Put the knife on the right side of the plate with its blade facing inward, and set the soupspoon to the right of the knife. Put the dessert fork above the plate, parallel to the edge of the table and with its handle pointing to the left; above it, put the dessertspoon with its handle pointing to the right. If space is tight, bring the dessert implements out with the course.

Put a bread plate above the forks and lay a butter knife across its upper rim. Arrange glassware in a diagonal line starting above the knife, going up and to the left in order of use from closest to farthest. Set out a wineglass for each type of wine you will be serving, and at the upper-left end of the diagonal, a water glass.

The Buffet

Choose a table or sideboard to use for the buffet, and arrange your serving dishes on it ahead of time to make sure the space will comfortably accommodate them. If possible, move the table away from the wall so guests can access both sides. Set the dinner plates at the end where the guests will start, and the napkins and silverware—if not set on the table—at the other end, so guests won't have to juggle too many items while serving themselves. Put cold dishes before hot ones, using trivets as needed. Check to ensure that each dish has its own appropriate serving utensil. In the remaining space, add a few decorative elements, such as candles or a seasonal arrangement of flowers or greenery that ties in with the table centerpiece.

Informal table setting: Everyday flatware, a plain white plate, and an all-purpose glass for water or wine. Place mats can stand in for a tablecloth.

Formal table setting: Special-occasion flatware and an optional charger. Wine and water glasses are arranged at an angle above the knife.

INDEX

ACKNOWLEDGMENTS

WELDON OWEN wishes to thank the following individuals and organizations for their kind assistance: Desne Ahlers, Teri Bell, Heather Belt, Carrie Bradley, Sarah Putman Clegg, Ken DellaPenta, Chris Hemesath, Sarah Mattern, Renée Meyers, Steve Siegelman, Sharon Silva, Nancy Wong, The Blackwell Files, Kelly Bogardus, Nils and Jennifer DeMatran, Greg and Aimee Price, Rod and Becker Rougelot, Bernardo Urquieta, and Suzanne Wood.

GEORGE DOLESE would like to thank Elisabet der Nederlanden for her continued loyalty and calming presence, Ansellmo Valte for helping out in the kitchen and advice on wine, and Ver Brugge Meat for quality product and friendly service.

SARA SLAVIN wishes to extend a special thanks to Sue Fisher King and Dandelion, both in San Francisco.

PHOTO CREDITS

QUENTIN BACON, all photography, except for the following:

JIM FRANCO: Pages 10 and 136 (left)

FREE PRESS

A Division of Simon & Schuster, Inc.

1230 Avenue of the Americas

New York, NY 10020

A WELDON OWEN PRODUCTION

First printed in 2005

Printed in China

FREE PRESS and colophon are registered trademarks of
Simon & Schuster, Inc.

For information regarding special discounts for bulk
purchases, please contact Simon & Schuster Special Sales
at 1 800 456 6798 or business@simonandschuster.com

Printed by Midas Printing Limited

10 9 8 7 6 5 4 3 2 1

Library of Congress Cataloging-in-Publication Data is available.

ISBN-13: 978-0-7432-7851-5

ISBN-10: 0-7432-7851-8

Jacket Images

Front cover: Campari and Soda, page 41.
Back cover: Champagne Cocktail, page 63; Rosehip Centerpiece,
page 102; Goat Cheese and Shallot Toasts, page 123.

THE ENTERTAINING SERIES

Conceived and produced by Weldon Owen Inc.

814 Montgomery Street, San Francisco, CA 94133

Telephone: 415-291-0100 Fax: 415-291-8841

In Collaboration with Williams-Sonoma, Inc.
3250 Van Ness Avenue, San Francisco, CA 94109

WILLIAMS-SONOMA, INC.
Founder & Vice-Chairman: Chuck Williams

WELDON OWEN INC.

Chief Executive Officer: John Owen

President and Chief Operating Officer: Terry Newell

Chief Financial Officer: Christine E. Munson

VP International Sales: Stuart Laurence

Creative Director: Gaye Allen

Publisher: Hannah Rahill

Associate Publisher: Amy Marr

Art Director: Nicky Collings

Designer: Rachel Lopez

Associate Editor: Donita Boles

Editorial Assistant: Juli Vendzules

Production Director: Chris Hemesath

Color Specialist: Teri Bell

Production and Reprint Coordinator: Todd Rechner

Associate Food Stylist: Elisabet der Nederlanden

Photographer's Assistant: Brooke Buchanan

Assistant Prop Stylists: Amy Heine, Shashona Burke

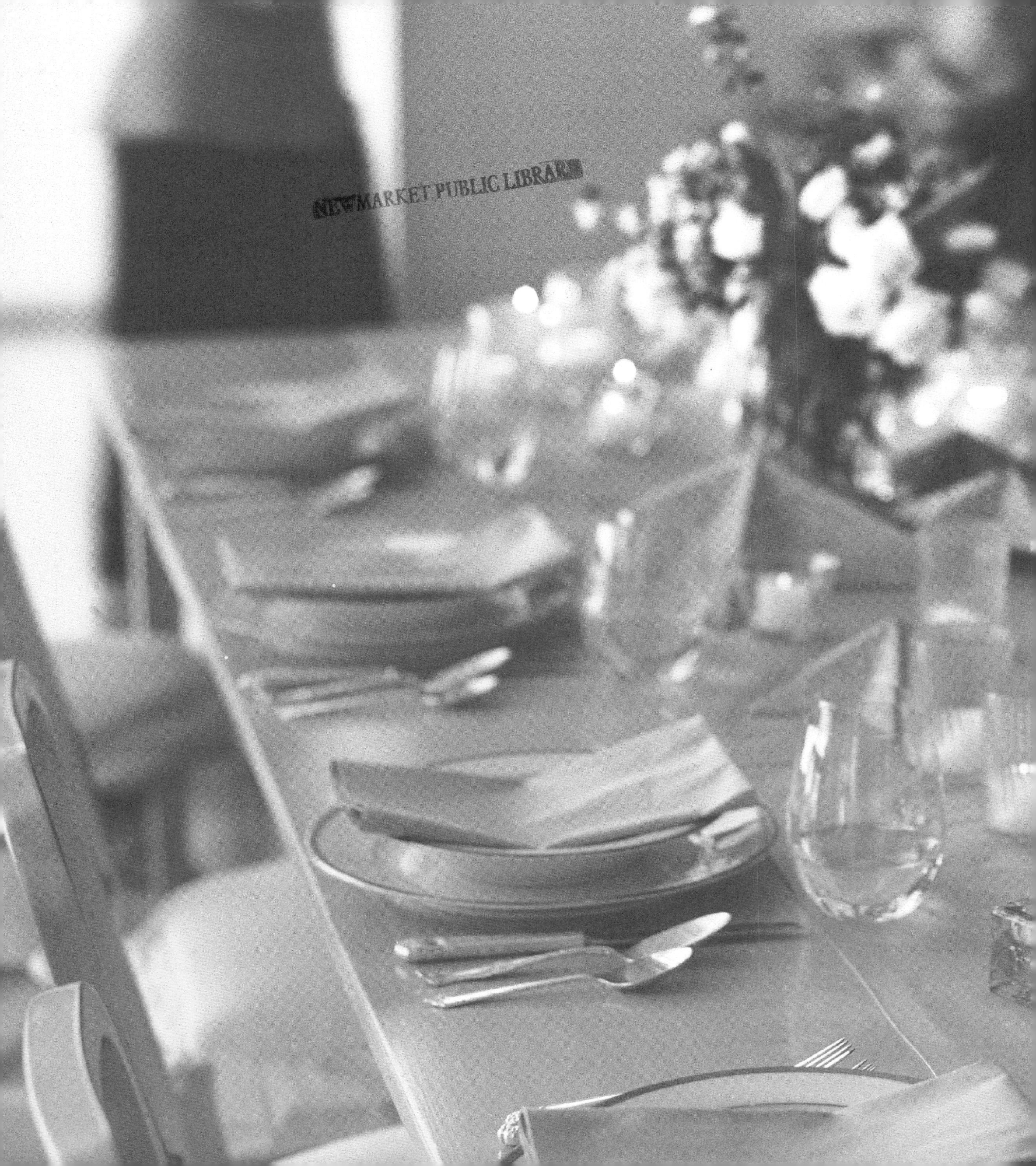